The Clothed Body

WITHDRAWN

WITHDRAWN

WITHDRAWN

Dress, Body, Culture

Series Editor: Joanne B. Eicher, *Regents' Professor, University of Minnesota*

Advisory Board:
Ruth Barnes, *Ashmolean Museum, University of Oxford*
Helen Callaway, *CCCRW, University of Oxford*
James Hall, *University of Illinois at Chicago*
Beatrice Medicine, *California State University, Northridge*
Ted Polhemus, *Curator, "Street Style" Exhibition, Victoria and Albert Museum*
Griselda Pollock, *University of Leeds*
Valerie Steele, *The Museum at the Fashion Institute of Technology*
Lou Taylor, *University of Brighton*
John Wright, *University of Minnesota*

Books in this provocative series seek to articulate the connections between culture and dress which is defined here in its broadest possible sense as any modification or supplement to the body. Interdisciplinary in approach, the series highlights the dialogue between identity and dress, cosmetics, coiffure and body alternations as manifested in practices as varied as plastic surgery, tattooing, and ritual scarification. The series aims, in particular, to analyze the meaning of dress in relation to popular culture and gender issues and will included works grounded in anthropology, sociology, history, art history, literature, and folklore.

ISSN: 1360-466X

Previously published in the Series

Helen Bradley Foster, *"New Raiments of Self": African American Clothing in the Antebellum South*
Claudine Griggs, *S/he: Changing*
Michaele Thurgood Haynes, *Dressing Up Debutantes: Pageantry and Glitz in Texas*
Anne Brydon and Sandra Niessen, *Consuming Fashion: Adorning the Transnational Body Sex and Changing Clothes*
Dani Cavallaro and Alexandra Warwick, *Fashioning the Frame: Boundaries, Dress and the Body*
Judith Perani and Norma H. Wolff, *Cloth, Dress and Art Patronage in Africa*
Linda B. Arthur, *Religion, Dress and the Body*
Paul Jobling, *Fashion Spreads: Word and Image in Fashion Photography*
Fadwa El Guindi, *Veil: Modesty, Privacy and Resistance*
Thomas S. Abler, *Hinterland Warriors and Military Dress: European Empires and Exotic Uniforms*
Linda Welters, *Folk Dress in Europe and Anatolia: Beliefs about Protection and Fertility*
Kim K.P. Johnson and Sharron J. Lennon, *Appearance and Power*
Barbara Burman, *The Culture of Sewing*
Annette Lynch, *Dress, Gender and Cultural Change*
Antonia Young, *Women Who Become Men*
David Muggleton, *Inside Subculture: The Postmodern Meaning of Style*
Nicola White, *Reconstructing Italian Fashion: America and the Development of the Italian Fashion Industry*
Brian J. McVeigh, *Wearing Ideology: The Uniformity of Self-Presentation in Japan*
Shaun Cole, *Don We Now Our Gay Apparel: Gay Men's Dress in the Twentieth Century*
Kate Ince, *Orlan: Millennial Female*
Nicola White and Ian Griffiths, *The Fashion Business: Theory, Practice, Image*
Ali Guy, Eileen Green and Maura Banim, *Through the Wardrobe: Women's Relationships with their Clothes*
Linda B. Arthur, *Undressing Religion: Commitment and Conversion from a Cross-Cultural Perspective*
William J.F. Keenan, *Dressed to Impress: Looking the Part*
Joanne Entwistle and Elizabeth Wilson, *Body Dressing*
Leigh Summers, *Bound to Please: A History of the Victorian Corset*
Paul Hodkinson, *Goth: Identity, Style and Subculture*
Michael Carter, *Fashion Classics from Carlyle to Barthes*
Sandra Niessen, Ann Marie Leshkowich and Carla Jones, *Re-Orienting Fashion: The Globalization of Asian Dress*
Kim K. P. Johnson, Susan J.Torntore and Joanne B. Eicher, *Fashion Foundations: Early Writings on Fashion and Dress*
Helen Bradley Foster and Donald Clay Johnson, *Wedding Dress Across Cultures*
Charlotte Suthrell, *Unzipping Gender: Sex, Cross-Dressing and Culture*
Yuniya Kawamura, *The Japanese Revolution in Paris Fashion*
Ruth Barcan, *Nudity: A Cultural Anatomy*

DRESS, BODY, CULTURE

Property of
FRA Library

00004785

The Clothed Body

WITHDRAWN

FASHION RETAIL
ACADEMY

Library

Renewals: 020 7307 2365   Email: library@fra.ac.uk

WITHDRAWN

15 Gresse Street, London W1T

 B

Oxford • New York

WITH

0000197 1 ✓

English edition
First published in 2004 by
Berg
Editorial offices:
First Floor, Angel Court, 81 St Clements Street, Oxford OX4 1AW, UK
175 Fifth Avenue, New York, NY 10010, USA

© Patrizia Calefato 2004

Paperback edition reprinted 2005

All rights reserved.
No part of this publication may be reproduced in any form
or by any means without the written permission of Berg.

Berg is the imprint of Oxford International Publishers Ltd.

Library of Congress Cataloging-in-Publication Data
Calefato, Patrizia.
    [Moda, corpo, mito. English]
    The clothed body / Patrizia Calefato ; English translation by Lisa Adams.
        p. cm. — (Dress, body, culture, ISSN 1360-466X)
    Includes bibliographical references.
    ISBN 1-85973-800-1 (cloth) — ISBN 1-85973-805-2 (pbk.)
1. Clothing and dress—Social aspects. 2. Fashion—Social aspects.
3. Body, Human—Social aspects. I. Title. II. Series.
    GT525.C3613 2004
    391—dc22   2004006547

British Library Cataloguing-in-Publication Data
A catalogue record for this book is available from the British Library.

ISBN 1 85973 800 1 (Cloth)
      1 85973 805 2 (Paper)

Typeset by Avocet Typeset, Chilton, Aylesbury, Bucks
Printed in the United Kingdom by Biddles Ltd, King's Lynn.

www.bergpublishers.com

Acknowledgements

I would like to thank my translator, Lisa Adams, who has worked with me, patiently and diligently, for many years. Lisa read English and French at Bristol University and History of Art at the Courtauld Institute London, completing her studies in Venice and Rome. She lives and works in Italy as a translator and editor.

I would also like to thank the photographer Marcus Pummer, who has kindly offered one of his lovely photos for the cover of this book. Mark lives and works in Vienna, and I have had occasion to become familiar with his work through the magazine 'Carnet', on which we both collaborate.

Contents

Introduction

An image in Marguerite Duras' novel *L'amant* is particularly striking in that it manages to convey the ability of a garment or an accessory to transform both a body and an identity, to challenge nature, as it were. The image is that of the adolescent heroine who dons a man's hat of 'rosc-coloured felt with a flat brim and a wide black band'. The hat acts upon her as a veritable instrument of change, a bridge between herself and the world:

> I tried on that hat, just for a laugh; I looked at myself in the shop mirror and saw, under that man's hat, the awkward skinniness of my frame, defect of my age, become something else. It ceased to be a crude and fatal fact of nature and became the opposite, a choice running counter to nature, a choice of the spirit. I see myself as another, as another would see me, from the outside, available to all, exposed to everyone's gaze, let loose in a circuit of cities, streets and pleasures. I buy the hat. I shall wear it always. Now that I own a hat that completely trans-forms me, I'll never abandon it. (Duras, 1985: 18–19)

The hat is the opposite of nature: it modifies artificially her slender frame, which the heroine sees as a defect of her age. The hat is a choice of the spirit, a conscious sign, even though donned casually at first, almost as a joke, as part of the narcissistic and carnivalesque enjoyment all teenagers feel when they put on strange garments and parade them in front of the mirror. This pleasurable sensation prompts the young girl to make the hat her inseparable companion; it becomes an emblem of her transformation into something other than what she felt herself to be before, a sort of ini-tiatory fetish towards a new identity. She likes the fact that wearing the hat exposes her to the gaze of others, a gaze which immediately turns her into another, as if she were looking at herself from the outside, as if the imper-fect beauty with which the hat endows her has laid open her body to a kind of metamorphosis.

This image of an adolescent girl in Indo-China may be taken as a metaphor for that particular synergy of signs and senses which the prac-tice of dressing has always produced. A garment exposes the body to a continuous transformation, organizing in signs – that is, in culture – what the natural world possesses as mere potential, as the tendency of the sensible to become significant. Even though we may not often think about it, dressing has to do with feeling pleasure and with recognizing that such pleasure consists in transforming nature, in 'working' it semiotically.

True, a garment can also 'cage' the body, condemning it to the forced task of representing a social role, position or hierarchy. In the history of dress, military, school and prison uniforms are examples of how clothing can be a controlling device for the body, sanctioning a closed system of correspondences between external appearance and social order. Yet everyone wears a uniform at one time or another, even those who think they have gained freedom of choice or social recognition with the first 'tribal' object they put on, whether it be a leather jacket or a Rolex. Ever since fashion has become a veritable syntax of that complex body language we call dress – or, as Barthes says, 'vêtement' – we are all familiar with the sense of alienation from one's own body which dressing according to a system of socially controlled images induces.

Yet at the heart of even the most *prêt-à-porter* and 'mass' gesture of choosing our wardrobe from a serial repetition of fashion images, an archetypal, carnivalesque gesture survives, which consists in disguise, masquerade, 'writing' the body and writing on the body, so that it becomes part of 'a circuit of ... streets and pleasures': our body for others and for ourselves as others. A gesture of profound joy and delight, of pleasure in masquerade, and sensual enjoyment. A synaesthetic game.

The clothed body expresses the way in which a subject is in and of the world through his/her aesthetic and physical appearance, his/her relation with other bodies and lived bodily experiences (see Calefato 1986, 1996); and so it can be considered a vehicle of desire, like the image of the young girl with the hat, to which she attributes the task of ensuring her rite of passage into the world. Her hat is not a uniform, however; it is not the sanctioned habit of the social group to which she belongs, but rather a matter of personal taste, of stylistic choice, or as Duras herself says, "an unusual, unexpected note". In the period and place where the heroine lived, no girl, no woman ever wore a man's hat. Her eccentric gesture thus upsets the norm, the unexpected intervenes to regulate taste and act as a unique, non-stereotypical pleasure and beauty principle through which the subject is transformed and exposed to the world.

At the root of clothing the body there may indeed be the unexpected, even though the study of costume and fashion does not always include the eccentric and sensual dimension of dress. Costume, above all traditional folk costume, tends to be static and to display an exact correspondence between signs and their social significance in relation to the person who wears them. Fashion, above all fashion in the age of its 'maturity', in our age of general serial repetition, often has to do with stereotypes, whether of an average notion of beauty, sexual gender or social roles. Fashion as image and as a system conveyed through images (photography, film, television, internet) is the place of imitation *par excellence*, the place where identity has strictly to do with repetition. And yet, one may glimpse in both costume and fashion signs with which the body is presented and enters into social communication, not through the image of corpse-like rigidity which so frightened Walter Benjamin in the fashion system, but rather through unexpected, non-replicant and sentient forms.

This book sets out to explore the phenomenology of dress through manifestations of the fashions and 'modes' which the body assumes, especially in contemporary reality. The approach is both subjective and discursive, while the methodology is not limited to a particular discipline, though a socio-semiotic bias is favoured, due to the profoundly subjective nature of the themes dealt with. The result is a strange polyphony, through which the author seeks to investigate how we make sense of the world and stimulate our senses, both when we put on "borrowed robes" and when we wear our own. Clothes as conveyors of meaning and value, that give shape to a system of objects in which the body finds the space for innumerable and complex sensorial identities.

Dress, Language and Communication

In the *Tractatus logico-philosophicus*, Wittgenstein proposes a clothing metaphor for language:

> Language disguises the thought, so that from the external form of the clothes one cannot infer the form of the thought they clothe, because the external form of the clothes is constructed with quite another object than to let the form of the body be recognized (Wittgenstein, 1922. Proposition 4.002).

Language, thought and dress are here associated and clothing is explicitly considered as a kind of bodily disguise, just as language is a disguise for thought. Language and dress are sign systems through which, Wittgenstein seems to be saying, what counts is not so much what is 'underneath', but rather the surface as such, the system or pattern itself which body and thought assume. The form of 'clothed thought' would thus be language, just as the garment is the form of the clothed body. Though perhaps not in Wittgenstein's intentions, in a more widely accepted sense today, the word 'language' does not simply refer to a verbal system, but involves all those sign systems with which human beings give shape to their relation to the world (see Ponzio, Calefato, Petrilli 1994: 58). Like language in this sense, dress functions as a kind of 'syntax', according to a set of more or less constant rules, depending on whether we are dealing with traditional costume or fashion. These rules allow a garment, and body coverings in general, to acquire meaning, whether that of a veritable social significance, codified in costume through time, or a pure and simple exhibition of interconnected signs on the body following associative criteria established by the fashion system.

Returning to Wittgenstein's metaphor and recalling how important the pictorial dimension of language is in the *Tractatus* – that is, its capacity to depict a fact (a 'state of things') through a system of images[1] – we may reflect on how the language of the clothed body shapes the body into a kind of map. Indeed, a sign-image is such in virtue of the connection between its various elements, each of which makes sense on the basis of its position in a given sequence. It is this position which allows a sign to represent something else.

One such example concerns a particular form of body covering, indeed one of the most ancient and archetypal: tattooing. The structural anthropologist Claude Lévi-Strauss has shown that in many societies not only does tattooing have a special social significance, but it also contains messages with a spiritual purpose (Lévi-Strauss 1958: 288). The social and aesthetic significance of tattooing as a sign-image – observed by Lévi-Strauss in the Maori of New Zealand – may be better understood if one considers the effect of 'doubling' the face and body, which are decorated as if they had been split in two. According to Lévi-Strauss the decoration *is* the face, or rather, it *creates* it (1958: 289), thereby conferring on the face social identity, human dignity and spiritual significance. The dual representation of the face, as depicted by the Maori, is indicative of a more profound doubling: that of the 'dumb' biological individual and the social personage that s/he has the task of embodying (Lévi Strauss 1958: 289). Thus the sign-picture or the sign-tattoo on the face has meaning not in virtue of the single graphic marks, but rather on the basis of the opposition-association set up between the two parts of the face or body, the actual one and the painted or incised one.

Another example concerns what Hebdige (1979: 102) calls the *bricolage* of subcultural styles: the composition or arrangement on the body of a collection of apparently incongruous objects, which taken as a whole create for the subject who wears them an organized and meaningful system analogous to the world (see Calefato 1996: 5–6, 15–16). The Mod's starched white collar and black tie, for instance, or the Punk's skin-piercing safety pin are pieces of a subcultural *bricolage* emphasizing the sign-role – 'unnatural' by definition – that banal, everyday objects assume when collocated in unusual places. The sign-value of these objects depends on their collocation in a network or 'web' of meanings. So, a sort of body 'cartography' is drawn on social territory, where each sign has a precise value according to its position.

Bodily coverings, clothes and skin decorations 'create' the body, shaping it together with the surrounding world. What we might call the 'degree zero' of clothing, the naked body, is itself replete with significance, since it is either the result of a significant absence, as Barthes says,[2] or a construction permeated with meaning and value (the body incised, tattooed, tanned, wrinkled, scarred, exposed beneath transparent garments, etc).

But now let's look at what covering oneself out of a 'sense of modesty' means. According to Sartre, it indicates the specifically human ability to be a *pure subject* (Sartre 1943: 363), by disguising the objectivity of the naked body exposed to the gaze and exhibiting, instead, our ability to see without being seen. Being a subject means, in this sense, recognizing that clothes have specific functions and dressing in order to convey a specific meaning, including the social meaning attributed to the notion of modesty. Moreover, in the case of costume (including uniform), functions are related to those aspects which make bodily coverings the sign of a person's age, social or sexual role, political career, and so on.

In an essay not included in *The Fashion System* Barthes identifies an axiological function in costume, its ability to produce social values that bear witness to the creative power of society over itself (1998: 74). Barthes makes an important distinction between costume and dress: while the former is an institutional, essentially social reality, independent of the individual, the latter is a unique reality through which the individual enacts on him/herself the general institution of costume (1998: 66). While dress, or attire, can be the object of psychological or morphological research, costume, as Barthes says, is the true object of sociological and historical research (1998: 67). Moreover, Barthes maintains that the dichotomy between costume and dress mirrors the Saussurian articulation of language into *langue* and *parole*: the former, a social institution, the latter, an individual act. The similarity with the linguistic sphere basically concerns the social value of clothing as a generic group, that is, a combination of costume and dress, corresponding to *language* in the Saussurian sense (1998: 66).

Barthes collocates fashion within the phenomenon of costume, though at times it oscillates between costume and dress, with an effect of mutual contamination: for instance, *haute couture* may use a traditional costume in the creation of a unique garment, and women's fashion may diversify the uniformity of costume depending on the occasion; whereas men's fashion tends towards dandyism, that is, it tends to emphasize the *manner* of wearing a standard outfit (1998: 68–9).

For Barthes fashion is much more than an occasion to demonstrate how a system analogous to language functions. Rather, as Gianfranco Marrone says, fashion is an emblem of our 'progressive awareness of the indissoluble bond between sign and society, semiology and sociology' (Marrone 1998: 77). The history of costume, Barthes says, has a general epistemological value, whereby with 'history of costume' he means a socio-semiotic reading of the phenomenon of clothing as an articulate language through which it is possible to analyse a culture as system and process, institution and individual act, expressive reserve and significant order (1998: 73).

The articulation of clothing into costume and dress – corresponding to *langue* and *parole* – is further developed by Barthes (1998: 73) with reference to one of the founders of structural phonology, N.S. Trubeckoj, who proposes as part of the phenomenon of dress 'the individual dimension of a garment, and how dirty or worn-out it is' and as part of the phenomenon of costume 'the difference, no matter how slight, between a young girl's garments and those of a married woman in certain societies' (Trubeckoj 1939 cited by Barthes 1998: 80). Barthes extends this opposition by considering, as part of the phenomenon of dress, how untidy a garment is, what it lacks, how it fits and how it is worn (crooked buttons, sleeves too long, etc), improvised clothing, colour (except in special circumstances, like mourning), and the characteristic gestures of the wearer. As part of the phenomenon of costume, on the other hand, Barthes proposes ritualized forms, materials and colours, fixed usages and, more generally, all those systems regulated by conformity and compatibility, the outer limits of which are represented by costumes for specific purposes, as in film and theatre (1998: 80). In the light of this classification it is interesting to note how fashion – which we include in costume – has paradoxically appropriated usages and forms which Barthes included in dress.

Let's look at these aspects one by one. When a garment is made to measure it is certainly unique, though with the invention of standard sizes, the body has been squeezed into numerical limits. A worn-out garment may have a sentimental value for its wearer, but as 'second-hand' it becomes a fashion item; and the same goes for the vogue for faded or ripped jeans. Untidiness and dirtiness may be part of the phenomenon of anti-fashion or urban tribal forms. The absence of a garment may be the sign of a collective use made of costume: for instance, feminist bra-burning in the 1960s, or Sharon Stone without underpants in *Basic Instinct*, which becomes a sign of the protagonist's sexual ambiguity. Eccentricities in how a garment is worn, on the other hand, concern everyday fashions: the vogue for buttoning jackets crookedly, wearing sleeves that are too long, or deliberately creased, unironed clothes, a vogue recently taken up by high fashion. Gesture and movement, too, in wearing certain garments, are often indicative of socially produced attitudes: for instance, the fashion dictate of narrow skirts or high heels that impose on women fixed, even stereotyped, movements when seated or walking.

According to Lotman (1993), fashion introduces a dynamic principle into seemingly immobile, everyday spheres. Traditional costume tends to maintain such spheres unchanged through time, while fashion tends to transmit signals which are antithetical to the everyday: capricious, voluble, strange, arbitrary, unmotivated, these are the terms we normally associate with fashion. So fashion becomes part of the image of a topsy-turvy world, where a tension is set up between the stability of the everyday, on the one hand, and the search for novelty and extravagance, on the other.

There is thus a structural difference between costume and fashion with regard to time – the stability and immutability of costume as opposed to the giddiness of fashion – and metaphorical space – a normal versus a topsy-turvy world. This difference directly concerns the social function of clothes: costume establishes a close relation between the individual and the community to which s/he belongs, while a fashionable garment has, by definition, a cosmopolitan status, even though its style may be inspired by 'ethnic' or traditional costume.

Let's take as an example some aspects related to the social significance of colour. Black, associated with mourning in the traditional costume of certain societies, has the ritual function (Bogatyrëv 1937) of associating the nothingness into which the body of the defunct has passed with the meaningless state in which the bereaved person finds him/herself. In virtue of its magical function, on the other hand, the use of black is forbidden for the garments of new-born babies, who are thereby protected from images associated with night, death and demons. Black, therefore, in the context of a traditional, symbolic concept of clothing as costume, is always associated with a specific, yet timeless, function, the significance of which is inscribed in 'languages' which, while different, are nevertheless morphologically enduring and belong to the universal phenomenon of myth enacted within a context of social relativism (Greimas 1976). This concerns both the way in which so-called archaic societies function and the extent to which the functional dimension of a garment persists even in mass, industrial sectors of social reproduction (the wedding dress, for instance).

In fashion, which is characteristic of social reproduction in the modern age, especially mass reproduction today, the social significance of colour is dispersed in a multiplicity of languages which, in turn, become social discourses (Greimas 1976). Fashion uses black, for instance, in various contexts and discourses: urban tribal styles, such as Punks and Goths; intersemiotic strategies between fashion and cinema (the role of black in *The Blues Brothers* or *Men in Black*); 'designer styles' (the use of black in Yamamoto, Versace or Dolce & Gabbana) (see Calabrese 1992); *bricolage* fetishes, and so on.

Take the wedding dress as a further example, the ritual function of which is subordinated to the mutability of fashion. The dress itself may be decontextualized, white being replaced by 'provocative' colours (such as red) and shapes (low-cut bodices, short skirts, etc).

The objects generated by the discourses of fashion are no longer, therefore, products of a collective expressiveness – myths in the traditional sense – but are rather signs of a style, and consumer objects. In other words, they become myths in the contemporary sense.

Rossi-Landi defines society as 'the aspect that material assumes on a human level' (1985: 32). And the sign dimension of society has characterized the history itself of cultures and civilizations. For instance, natural languages are transcribed as signs, and the sociolinguistic categories underlying them are too, by nature, signs. We might also adduce the symbolic function of non-verbal sign systems, like food and clothing. Sign systems, in which costume and fashion are included, manifest their functional mechanisms as generators of relations between individuals, devices for shaping the world and sources of meaning and value. It is in this sense that sign systems may be called communication systems. In the chapter entitled *Schema di riproduzione sociale* of his book *Metodica filosofica e scienza dei segni* Rossi-Landi defines communication as social reproduction (1985: 27–45), that is, as the whole context of the production-exchange-consumption of commodities and messages, all considered signs on the basis of his 'homological method'. It is not only the moment of exchange that involves the communicative dimension – expressed as techniques of persuasion in advertising, marketing strategies, etc – but production and consumption as well. This is especially evident in our 'post-industrial' age. The manifestations of sign production-communication go from the telecommunications industry, information technology and cinema to automation and educational systems. Consumption as communication includes, moreover, the use of telephones, electronic gadgets, computers, televisions, satellites, and should be considered in the light of its so-called 'fluidity', that is, its mobile, flexible and hybrid character (see Lee 1993: 254–9).

Today production, exchange and consumption are three virtually simultaneous moments: Rossi-Landi alludes to their structural similarity, which establishes a set of resemblances within social production itself, particularly at a level of 'global production'.[3] This regards the fact that a given artefact, whether verbal or non-verbal, makes explicit, 'recounts' as it were, the whole production process – language, culture, the human race even – that has generated it. Many contemporary signs-commodities – jeans, Coca-Cola, credit cards – make explicit the globalized social reproduction of which they are the result and within which they are exchanged and consumed. The particular socio-semiotic characteristic of such signs-commodities is that of containing within themselves a communicative value, of being communication *tout court*, whether they are produced, exchanged or consumed.

The proximity of signs and commodities[4] means that the latter's value is considered, above all, in terms of social relations. Today, in an age of 'total' communication, these relations imply that the value of an object consists not so much in its function – its usefulness – or in what it is worth, in the traditional sense, as in its communicative value, measurable in terms of speed and innovation.

The concept of innovation is much less arbitrary than it might at first seem. It concerns the universal sign quality of social reproduction, as several recent research projects have demonstrated.[5] A creative process, a service, a development programme, an object can all be called innovative, especially from a communicative perspective, if innovation is socially represented as such, if it is founded on social discourses that circulate and are reproduced both within restricted groups (a company, a public administration, a government) and extended, mass communities. In this sense, the 'authenticity' of the social discourse that sustains innovation is crucial. The discourse must circulate 'as if' it were true; it must respond to hidden meanings and expectations, construct life styles and interact with other discourses.

Yet, paradoxically, we may also speak of the 'destructive semiotic character'[6] of innovation: the fact that a consumer item, or indeed a production means, has become obsolete concerns depletion as a sign, not as a 'body'.[7] Discarding the old, and substituting it with the latest novelty, happens in every phase of social reproduction, in virtue of communication techniques that exploit 'total' signs: modularity, speed, design, virtuality, customization and so on. Endless examples could be taken from contemporary life: the philosophy underpinning the idea of software, the role of design in the car, hi-fi and electrical appliance industries, the concepts of time, space and the body in the use of mobile phones, and Web consumerism are just some examples.

Contemporary fashion acts as a paradigm in sign systems; it is, by definition, concerned with innovation, as demonstrated by Simmel (1895), who was one of the first to analyse the dialectic between innovation and imitation. The fashion system contains a mediation[8] between taste and received meaning, filtered through a special relation between sign, discourse and the sensible world.[9] In particular, fashion oscillates between an orientation towards the new and the immediate communicability of this 'new' as something which is socially approved and has the validity of an aesthetic absolute.

As Lotman (1993) says, fashion is collocated in the sphere of the unpredictable; what we might also call the sphere of imperfection,[10] a concept that makes explicit the way in which fashion manages to present itself both as an unexpected interruption of received meaning and its perennial reconstruction. What I have called 'mass fashion' (Calefato, 1996) is a complex system of images, words, objects and multilayered social discourses, all using a plurality of expressive forms: *haute couture* experiments in style, popular urban culture, everyday wear, and the clothing imagery that populates the intersection between fashion and cinema, fashion and music, fashion and design. The extent to which these discourses are perceived and reworked within the social sphere influences the relation between fashion and the sensible world, while the problem of 'sensing' and representing the world through dress, fashion and style becomes increasingly urgent.

This raises the interesting theoretical question of whether a sign system (in this case, fashion) models[11] the world as a *continuum*, an amorphous mass, 'Hamlet's cloud', or the world as a place in which the sensible is already manifest (Greimas 1970). These two theoretical approaches have traditionally been considered antithetical – for instance, in the field of the cognitive sciences – whereas they are actually parallel, one implying the other, if seen from the perspective of a social significance linked to taste and the senses. If there is a sense 'of the world' in fashion today, this can only consist in 'giving the word' to a world which is sentient but mute with regard to the unexpected, the unheard, the non-stereotypical. A world in which social reproduction is also essentially 'sign alienation';[12] that is, the stereotypical repetition of types of behaviour and images, filters so encrusted with sense and the senses that signs, especially visual signs, become imperatives.

Fashion, more especially its visual component, is communicated as the new, the unexpected, the unpredictable; but it is also, paradoxically, communicated through what Barthes calls the 'linguistic theft' of contemporary mythology. So, to what extent is the discourse of fashion, especially its visual dimension, reproduced in the form of sign alienation, or as Greimas (1995) would say, as a simulacrum of existence? To what extent do we perceive the clothed body, its form, its beauty, through the already-seen, the already-felt, through codified, obsolete roles, such as those connected with male and female stereotypes? Conversely, to what extent do the images and (not just visual) complexities of the fashion system transform, or disrupt, the existing order? To what extent do they display continual excess and turn aesthetics into a*esthesis* and social practice?

Notes

1. Wittgenstein 1922: Proposition 3: "The logical picture of the facts is the thought."
2. For instance, not wearing a tie; see Barthes *Scritti* (Ital trans 1998: 82).

3. See the chapter entitled *Omologia fra produzione linguistica e produzione materiale* in Rossi-Landi, 1985, especially the author's classification of the tenth and final level of what he calls "the production ... of utensils and statements".

4. Ross-Landi proposed this as early as the 1960s.

5. The European Commission's *Green Paper on Innovation* (1995) is a good example.

6. Paraphrasing Walter Benjamin in *Il carattere distruttivo* (Ital trans 1995).

7. On the distinction between sign and body see Rossi-Landi 1985: 137–66 *et passim* and Calefato 1997b: 12–13.

8. For socio-semiotics this mediation is typical of fashion.

9. Nearly half a century after the publication of *The Fashion System* it is now clear that for Barthes fashion was not simply writing about clothes, but as Gianfranco Marrone says "a type of discourse in which clothing practices, aesthetic representations and specialised utterances were combined in a complex form *of life*" (Marrone 1998).

10. Paraphrasing Greimas.

11. As language or *bricolage*.

12. Paraphrasing Rossi-Landi's "linguistic alienation".

2

Dress and Social Identity

In 1937 the Russian semiotician Pëtr Bogatyrëv, using a functionalist scheme, analysed the folk costume of Monrovia, in which he identified a series of functions: practical, aesthetic, magical and ritual. According to Bogatyrëv, even the smallest detail allows us to recognize the function to which a garment corresponds. For example, white for mourning dress alludes to a ritual function; red stripes on young girls' skirts, to a social function; red for young children's clothes is used to ward off evil spells and reflects a magical function. Every colour is related to the age and thus the social status of the individual in the community. This functionalist analysis foregrounds the symbolic significance of clothes: a garment is a sign, and wearing it fulfils specific functions that can coexist, or overlap, in the same item. When the dominant function is particularly strong, it neutralizes the others: for instance, the aesthetic overrides the practical function when the body is subjected to deformations or lacerations.

Bogatyrëv stresses a sort of closure in the way in which each function establishes the social significance of a garment, and he defines folk costume in general as a signifying system. Nevertheless, his analysis allows for an excess, so to speak: residual meanings expressed, above all, in the status of that most particular of functions, the aesthetic function. Just as what Jakobson (1963) calls the 'phatic function' in spoken language is there simply to maintain a minimum level of communication or contact between speakers (humanly more important than, for example, defining social status), the aesthetic function in the non-verbal language of folk costume indicates that signs are merely 'there' in clothes. Thus an 'unmotivated' relation is set up between body and garment, a 'something more' that exceeds functional equivalence. Even the signs that indicate functions other than the aesthetic (the colour or width of the stripes on the young girls' skirts, for example) and sanction the social importance of costume were originally based on aesthetic details: fabric, colour, shape, size, position (vertical, horizontal) and so on.

Bogatyrëv found a close analogy between folk costume and mother tongue, both of which he defines as systems having 'the function of a structure of functions' (1937: 140). We give emotional prominence to our mother tongue and national costume since they are nearest to us, writes Bogatyrëv. They create a concept of community for which we can use the possessive pronoun 'our': saying 'our language', 'our culture', 'our costume' gives an emotional colouring to these phenomena (1937: 142), due to the long and intimate coexistence established between them and the community. In this sense, folk costume, which is subjected to community censure, is the opposite of fashion: a garment subjected to rapidly changing tastes does not have time to bond permanently either with the collective social 'body' or any individual body (1937: 141).

Popular dress is part of an almost immutable community tradition, whereas fashionable dress is cosmopolitan. Nevertheless, fashion has often referred explicitly to the social imagery of a specific group or community, through the use of different 'texts'. Bogatyrëv maintains that a community invests folk costume with an emotional value. And this makes sense even today if we accept that fashion itself is a form of popular culture: it activates and draws on that complex area of social imagery in which folklore and images stratified in the collective memory coexist; in other words, texts in which the semiotic material is made up of different languages.

A good example is the role played by Southern Italy in the construction of fashion imagery. Dolce & Gabbana, Versace and many other Italian designers have recently interpreted this role by alluding in their collections to the part played by the South in shaping Italian cultural awareness, to which, since the end of the Second World War, not only literature and the fine arts, but also the mass media, including cinema and fashion, have all contributed. The male vest, Al Pacino style pin-striped suits, close-fitting white shirts, beachwear based on a *La Dolce Vita* ideal of male beauty are all aesthetic ideals coming from the Italian deep south.

Ideals of female beauty and fashion, too: the dark Mediterranean type epitomized by Sophia Loren and Anna Magnani, cloned today in various guises, wearing tight-fitting black bodices and long, full skirts, perhaps with white gym shoes and a headscarf, thick eyebrows, a full hour-glass figure, a trace of down on the upper lip. We're reminded of Stefania Sandrelli in *Sedotta e abbandonata*, together with all the women, whether real or imagined, who peopled the sun-drenched streets of Southern Italian towns forty years ago.

The resonance of such imagery, not just on the *haute couture* catwalk or in the designer's *atelier*, but also in our everyday choices, is certainly proof of how a community (in this case a nation) 'imagines itself' through a series of small, yet significant bonds and not just through economic or commercial pacts. While the latter type of pact often leads to a selfish closure within the notion of 'identity', the bonds constructed by social imagery are open, 'contaminated', and tend not to be divisive. Anna Magnani's peasant gear mixes with Silvana Mangano's chic ankle socks,[1] while the plaits worn by Southern Italian woman to tame their abundance of thick, curly hair mix with the traditional thin plaits of African women living in Europe, now in vogue amongst western teenagers.

There is an ancient legend in Iceland that tells how the terrible Christmas Cat[2] will come and get you if you don't wear a new item of clothing at Christmas. This monster attacks the poorest people, those who haven't been able to find even the smallest of new objects to wear. For this reason it is customary for women to spin different coloured yarns to make a new garment, or just a new pair of socks, for their children at Christmas in order to protect them from the monster. The legend is also an explicit invitation to the rich to give at least one new item of clothing to the poor, who would otherwise suffer a terrible fate.

As with all legends it is difficult to know which came first, the tale or the custom. Does the desire to wear something new at Christmas spring from this legend? Or is the legend itself merely a culturally codified reflection of those rites of rebirth associated with the ancient pagan significance of this festival? Clothes are our second skin, and what better meaning to give them on this occasion than that of a visible renewal and rebirth, made possible for everyone, even those who can't afford a new garment.

Even our post-industrial rites of Christmas consumerism find their *raison d'être* in this everyday ritual. Otherwise, how could they have such a strong grip on our imagination, if they were not part of some distant, buried memory of authentic gestures? And fashion, too, plays the same game, offering us the chance to dress up for the occasion and, like the Icelandic legend, telling us that even one small new object is enough to inscribe the festivities on our body.

Fashion seems to have fully assimilated the modern connotation of Christmas, given the widespread tendency to reflect, literally, its festive symbolism in clothes. Colour, for instance, has always had an important symbolic value in the history of costume, especially in Christmas attire. Significantly the dominant colour on this occasion is red, traditionally associated with pagan rites of fertility, (re)birth and sun-worship. Shoes, stockings and garments of every description combine their aesthetic function (of adorning the body as a source of light, like the sun) with the magical function, often attributed to the colour red in folk costume, of warding off evil spirits.

This ritual of dressing up for Christmas extends to the more worldly New Year's festivities, where, to welcome in the new year, red often appears in that 'low' garment, close to the body's erogenous zones. The habit of wearing red underwear, which has no significant precedence in popular dress prior to the modern age, suggests that clothes still have a magical function today. Red – the colour of blood, source of life – is auspicious for the new year and, at the same time, offers an occasion for an implicit seduction rite, allowing both sexes to reveal that they are wearing something red underneath.[3] This innocent erotic game merges with the surreal power of contemporary fashion, which consists in overturning, literally, the order of bodily coverings, exhibiting what is normally hidden and putting what is underneath on top.

The new technological materials,[4] too, are well suited to our glittering Christmas attire: clothes made of these materials seem straight out of a NASA laboratory, or inspired by the magical PVC costume created by Ferragamo for the Good Fairy in Andy Tennant's *Cinderella* (Museo Salvatore Ferragamo 1998: 80–81). Garments that create a *trompe l'oeil* effect similar to a hologram, and clothed bodies as bright as Christmas trees; the tree as the sylvan double of the human body, bedecked with colour and light at Christmas, as if it were a body totem to propitiate.

In Northern Europe, on the feast of St Lucy's Day (13 December), images of the saint show her bearing gifts, dressed in brilliant white with glowing candles on her head. This visible resplendence inverts the condition of the saint's blindness[5] and so light becomes a metaphor for the magico-religious illumination of body and mind.

The 'garment of light' (like the *traje de luz* of the toreros) is a classic example of a costume replete with ritual significance, through which magic is reproduced in everyday practices. So dressing up for Christmas could be seen not merely as a vain and futile consumer whim, but rather as a way to embody, literally, certain values in order to escape from the terrible Christmas Cat, emblem of the dark fate awaiting all those who haven't the will, or the means, to renew themselves at least once a year by shaking off stereotypes.

In Woody Allen's film *Deconstructing Harry* one of Harry's wives, the psychoanalyst interpreted in his fantasies by the lovely Demi Moore, has a religious crisis at a certain point in her life. From a sensual, liberal and worldly intellectual she becomes a strict Orthodox Jew. The change is made strikingly visible on her body: low-cut blouses, miniskirts and long, flowing hair are replaced by drab shawls, long skirts and neat hairdos.

Yet this austere 'Jewish look' that Woody Allen so irreverently pokes fun at is not his own invention. In 1998 the Israeli Amos Ben Naeh attempted to launch a *corpus* of fashion imagery inspired by religious orthodoxy.[6] The models in his agency lengthened their hems and sleeves, wore heavy stockings and buttoned-up, high-necked tops, covered their heads and tied back their hair. Orthodox Jewish culture thus set this rigid control of real and imaginary bodies against the invasive superabundance of images that construct beauty, especially female beauty, either in terms of unrestrained nudity or of clothing paradigms which are, at least apparently, free from restrictions and taboos.

The potential market for this new look was not just Israel. In both Europe and America post-Diaspora Judaism is largely made up of practising Jews who have presumably welcomed this mediation between religious dogma and the world of consumer advertising, from which their religion theoretically obliges them to keep their distance.[7]

Orthodoxy in fashion is not, however, the prerogative of Jewish culture alone. It finds a parallel in Islamic fundamentalism, which imposes equally severe prescriptions on its followers, especially women, concerning how to dress and appear in public. Indeed, in every culture there is a close relation between clothes and religious practices. Dressing means appearing, showing oneself to others, and the more the construction of one's self-image depends on the observance of religious dogma, the more it is concerned with how one exposes one's body to the public gaze.

Yet there is perhaps an even more profound aspect to clothing within a religious context, connected to its symbolic and mythological significance as a means of crossing the boundary between the human and the divine. The officiator of a cult who dons a religious vestment is at this boundary, and it is his/her clothed body that sanctions such a spatial-social collocation. Ancient initiation rites in many primitive cultures include a modification or transformation of the body through clothing, painting, feathering or tattooing.

The modern western view that integralist practices impose or inflict rigid dress codes on the body runs the risk of presumption in its claim to represent true freedom of dress.[8] Our judgement of the ancient Chinese practice of foot-binding, for example, or the use of the veil in Islam, or any other traditional form of covering the body in 'clothes of containment', often does not take into account even the more recent history of costume in which forms of secular fundamentalism have expressed themselves through dress.

In Nazi Germany, for example, Goebbels issued the order (in 1941) that all Jews wear a yellow star in order to distinguish them from the 'Aryans', while from a different point of view, the civilian uniform in Maoist China was an integralist sign, ideologically motivated by the necessity of creating social equality, even in terms of physical appearance. And today in that most eastern of western countries, Japan, wearing a uniform is a way of disciplining mind and body, especially in the younger generations, whose school uniforms are strictly regulated by age and sex. Even subculture styles that oblige members of urban tribes to follow precise dress codes, otherwise they run the risk of being outcast, are a secular reworking, in an urban consumer context, of ancient religious and social rituals of dress.

So in any discourse on clothing it is difficult to draw the line between an authentic freedom of dress and the rules and regulations (starting with fashion) that function as a kind of clothing syntax similar to that which governs language. In the modern age, whenever a political, social or religious élite has attempted to regulate or control the syntax of either language or clothing they have done so as part of a totalitarian regime (whether actual or planned). Persecuted groups have often been objects of manipulation and control, like the Jews in Nazi Germany, or women, whose presumed natural modesty is central to the look created by Ben Naeh.

Fashion and censorship have always been in conflict; the volatile, experimental nature of fashion often triggers off a hostile reaction from moralists against a new length, a new *look*, a new style, etc. Yet in the end the perverse mechanism of how fashions spread actually produces the opposite effect: a condemnation, not of the new, but of the old, whereby what is out-of-fashion becomes the butt of social censure. The relation between fashion and censure becomes even more complex when the former is circulated through the mass media: advertising and photography do not simply transcribe clothing signs into a propagandist and iconic language, but reinterpret, reformulate and exacerbate these signs, thereby creating a special genre of translation between different sign systems (inter-semiotic translation) and different text types (intertextual translation). The following are just some examples.

In the autumn of 1995 Calvin Klein launched an advertising campaign for a new collection of jeans, but then withdrew it almost immediately under attack from pressure groups like the American Family Association. According to his critics, the New York designer had committed an outrage that verged on an incitement to paedophilia: the new jeans were wore unbuttoned by a group of young teenagers who, at the same time, conspicuously showed off the designer's new collection of lingerie underneath.

Klein commented to the *New York Times*, when he announced the withdrawal of his campaign, that the ad was meant to convey that young people today were strong and independent-minded. Evidently this was not the interpretation given to the publicity message by family associations, sociologists and teachers, who clearly had never seen the multitudes of teenagers hanging out at school, on the street or in clubs dressed exactly like the youngsters in the Calvin Klein advertisement, well before it even came out. Perhaps not all with designer-label jeans and lingerie but free, nevertheless, to show off a pierced navel or simply to follow one of those street fashions that are transmitted like a sort of smoke-signal. The designer had done nothing more than pick up this smoke signal, using Steven Meisel's photographs, with their spare yet subtly erotic imagery.[9]

The scandal caused by the Klein-Meisel advertisement had the all-American flavour of a Manichean and superficial moralism, but it is, nevertheless, a good example of the tense relation that has always existed between fashion and censorship. Even more notorious, perhaps, is the Italian duo Benetton-Toscani, whose images of a terminal AIDS patient, a nun kissing a priest, and a black mother breast-feeding a white baby are just some examples of images which are regularly the target of moral censure and heated controversy. The accused, in this case, isn't a garment (Benetton-label items don't appear in the photos) but the metapublicity message, the image-signs that express something in themselves, apart from the implicit 'buy this label' message. The same thing happens with Calvin Klein, though in a less sophisticated way: here we actually see the jeans, but the metapublicity message appeals to styles and tastes that are already widespread; in other words, it communicates, not through ostentation, but through allusion and complicity.

Fashion shows are often the occasion for a chorus of censure against a recurrent style of women's clothes that alludes, deliberately and unequivocally, to pornography and prostitution, and so is seen as a harbinger of rampant licentiousness, not to mention being considered in sheer bad taste.[10] Yet the very next season we may witness a trend in the opposite direction: a look inspired by propriety and restraint. Clearly, here too we are dealing with a fashion metadiscourse: the desire to provoke a reaction in order to set up a self-referential discourse, by alluding to tastes and taboos already present in social imagery.

By contrast, the censorship campaign against the miniskirt in the 1960s had quite different implications: here conservatives and moralists were criticizing, not simulacra, but real live legs that had invaded the world of the public gaze. And the battle against this censorship had profound ethical implications, which coincided with a concerted affirmation of female freedom and narcissism in everyday life, not just in the photographer's studio or on the catwalk. This time fashion had something truly liberating to say. Indeed, the newly acquired sense of freedom inspired, in this case, by the miniskirt has often been associated with revolutionary changes in female dress (more so than in men's fashion). The last century has seen petticoats and corsets disappear, skirts get shorter, necklines plunge, colours get brighter and the advent of women's trousers.

Today the conflict between fashion and censure is above all a matter of style, that is, of the *forms* in which fashion manifests itself. Already in the 1980s Punk had implicitly grasped this change of emphasis. Punk style was deviant in the sense of putting the wrong thing in the wrong place: a safety pin in the nose, blue or green hair, or an obscene slogan on a T-shirt.

'Who loves me follows me,' a teenage backside in Italian 'Jesus' jeans could still say in the 1970s.[11] Follow, that is, a fashion, a backside, Jesus, or simply an image? The irony and ambiguity of the message created a scandal, but the image made history thanks to its grace and intelligence. Today we have few images to follow; it's rather images that follow us, and it is for this reason that censorship is no longer imaginatively or morally potent, and conveniently espouses the most bigoted forms of political correctness.

In the winter of 1993–94 French *haute couture* found itself in an embarrassing position with regard to the Islamic world. The Indonesian Council of *Ulema*[12] banned Chanel after designer Karl Lagerfeld used Koranic verses on the bodice of three dresses worn at the Paris fashion show by Claudia Schiffer. The French fashion house and Karl Lagerfeld in person immediately sent the Council an official apology, a necessary move since Chanel was quite interested in tapping the rich Arab market, which might well have withdrawn its custom after an incident of this kind. Market forces in this case turned out to be more important than artistic mannerisms. The *faux pas* was so clamorous that Chanel even had the garments in question destroyed, withdrew all photographic negatives of them and asked the photographers who had been at the fashion show to do the same.[13]

This was an exemplary incident, in which market forces, fashion and mutual respect between cultures all merged. For Islamic integralists Lagerfeld had obviously committed a sacrilege in mixing the profanity of the female body and the vulgar commercial object with the sacredness of the word of God. And yet combining clothes and writing is a deep-rooted practice in the aesthetics of fashion. In the West, if we were to see a T-shirt with 'Thou shalt have none other gods before me' written on it, we would simply think it was either a bit kitsch or a bit sanctimonious, whereas, in Islam, putting the words of the Koran on the bodice of a dress is considered no less than a wanton act of profanation.

Jewish tradition, on the other hand, has a law which sanctions dressing in scripture. Teffilin, strips of parchment that devout Jews wrap round their heads, cite passages from the Old Testament, and this ritual reflects a specific dogma in Exodus and Deuteronomy (Gandelman 1992). Yet think what an outcry there would be amongst the Jewish community if they were to see a phylactery inscribed with sacred Hebrew verses paraded on the head of a top model!

So was the *Ulema*'s condemnation simply an excess of fundamentalism, a kind of remake, in the history of fashion, of the censure against Salman Rushdie's *Satanic Verses*? The issue is a complex one. Is it right to offend other traditions in the name of aesthetic and economic freedom? And vice versa, could we not argue that Claudia Schiffer's bodice has the same communicative value today that a marvel like the Taj Mahal had in the past?

In the summer of 1994 the Italian Foreign Office refused to issue a diplomatic passport to a newly elected Euro-MP because it was thought that the photograph on it didn't correspond to the actual person. An incredible decision, since what made the photo an inadequate representation of the politician was the fact that he wasn't wearing a tie! The civil servants working in the diplomatic passports office maintained that the absence of a tie was sufficient to call the MP's personal identity into question. The tie thus assumed the role of a distinctive feature on the body, with the same status as a beard, hair colour, age, weight, glasses or plastic surgery. The affair concluded happily, thanks to a bit of mental elasticity on the part of the over-zealous civil servants, yet it is indicative of the fact that clothes now define not only personal, but also political identity.

We have all chanced to meet, at the seaside for example, someone we normally see only at work, and haven't recognized them immediately, since they were dressed (or undressed) differently. The same might happen with a soldier, policeman or nurse, whom we are used to seeing in uniform, and so we don't recognize them in 'plain clothes'. In the same way, the tie seems to have become part of a politician's uniform, without which he cannot be properly identified and, moreover, he may even be barred access to government institutions.

Today the image of public men and women is of paramount importance; a direct and inescapable relation has been set up between two languages – the language of dress and the language of politics. And this is reinforced by the fact that the language of politics is now primarily the language of television, where even before hearing what a politician has to say, we see his/her image, his/her clothed body, on the screen. Image-makers, who devote themselves to the private look of public figures, are everywhere, not just in the USA, where a politician's image, both public and private, has been in the limelight for decades. A passage in John Grisham's spy novel *The Pelican Brief* (1992) well illustrates this situation. The advisor of a fictional United States president urges him to wear a cardigan when he appears on television to comment on the murder of two members of the Supreme Court. The aim is to simulate a reassuring grandfatherly figure.

If television, or rather the exaggerated and mystifying use that politics makes of television, has replaced the mass political rallies held in the open air, if this lively electrical appliance has muddied the waters and created an excessive commingling of eye, ear and brain, then we mustn't forget that historically there has always been a close relation between politics and fashion. The famous case of the sobriquet *sans culottes* for French revolutionaries derives from the fact that they chose to wear long trousers, and so appeared 'sans culottes', that is, without the traditional garment worn by members of the *Ancien Régime*. Moreover, politics has often given names to fashions that spread far beyond restricted political groups: Imperial and Victorian styles are so-called after, respectively, the political regime and reign during which these dress styles were popular.

In rhetoric, a discourse genre called *oratio togata* recalls the oratorical style of those who wore the senatorial toga in ancient Rome. And here the relation between language, politics and dress is exemplary. Indeed, Marguerite Yourcenar claims that in her novel *Memoirs of Hadrian* (1951) she has the emperor speak in this way, because it embodies the ideal of masculine dignity in Classical Antiquity; and in support of this claim she adduces the image of the dying Caesar adjusting the folds of his toga.

The African-American scholar Cornel West (1993) has identified a similar ideal of dignity in the black suit and white shirt worn by Martin Luther King and Malcolm X as an affirmation of the seriousness and commitment of their fight for black civil rights.

In these last two examples the relation between fashion and politics is inverted: it is the politician or political stance that determines the dress code, not vice versa; it is the way of conceiving one's appearance style that dictates visibly the significance of a professional commitment. Here the politician isn't conforming to an already established dress code, wearing a uniform or simply wanting to look good on television, but is making an ethical choice that belittles any flattery or clever advice a style councillor might give. Instead of judging politicians on their 'top model' effect, as usually happens, why don't we try and guess which one of them, like Caesar, would think of adjusting his (or her) toga after being stabbed?

Notes

1. Silvana Mangano is an Italian actress from the 1950s.
2. A monster that, even for Icelanders, comes from the far frozen north.
3. Perhaps with unbuttoned jeans, or a slit skirt.

4. Translucent, transparent, changing colour depending on the light, or with mirror-like surfaces.

5. St Lucy is the patron saint of sight.

6. Amos Ben Naeh is an Orthodox Jew who runs the creative department of an advertising company in Israel.

7. This story could provide interesting material for the trenchant irony of an Italian Jewish intellectual like Moni Ovadia, who knows Jewish culture inside-out.

8. In the West the view still prevails that our world is, in some sense, more 'civilized'.

9. Madonna used Meisel's photographs for her eros-biography *Sex*.

10 Bras and corsets worn as over-garments, tango-style dresses, tight-fitting cardigans with double openings, skirts slit up to the navel, Salome-like transparent materials.

11. Photographed once again by Toscani.

12. The *Ulema* (singular *'Alim*) are the sages of Islam, those who possess the quality of *ilm*, instruction in the broadest sense. They are usually theologians, professors, judges or theorists of Islamic law, and in a Muslim state they form a council which has a role in government.

13. Lagerfeld had taken the incriminating text from a tomb inscription in the Taj Mahal at Agra, built in 1632 by the Mogul emperor Shah Janan in memory of his beloved wife, Arjumand Banu Begum, called Mumtaz Mahal, 'The Palace Favourite', who died in childbirth in 1631 after 20 years of inseparable companionship with the emperor. Lagerfeld mistakenly thought that the inscriptions were amorous verses, whereas they were, in fact, Koranic verses, which are often used as a decorative feature in Islamic architecture.

Style and Styles between Fashion and the Grotesque

3

What happens when we speak of style, when we use the word 'style', particularly in everyday language? We commonly use expressions like 'she's got style', 'it's a matter of style' or 'that's his style'. In all these cases the word 'style' immediately displays its semiotic status; it declares, if not exactly what is meant in each case, then the fact that we are in the presence of a system of intentional signs, with distinctive features, that are discontinuous with regard to a presumed naturalness or hypothetical degree zero of behaviour and language. Even when we use expressions like 'she has natural style', the opposition between the words 'style' and 'natural' only serves to highlight the declared unnaturalness of the concept of style.

When we speak of style our discourse involves not only aesthetic and formal appraisals, but also ethical considerations, relative to the meaningfulness, and not just the meaning, of traits we recognize as value-laden. The fact that these values are collocated outside prescriptive morals and aesthetics only enhances the 'semiotic grip' of style, since it demonstrates that our appraisals are collocated in an ideal universe where *obvious* meaning (as Barthes would say) is put aside and so-called *oblique* meaning (linked to taste and sensibility) is emphasized.

On the other hand, we mustn't ignore the more common meaning of style as 'an ensemble of formal traits that characterize a typologically and historically determined group of works' (Segre 1981: 549). In this sense the terms classical, baroque, Jugend and so on would be examples of how the concept of style corresponds to a kind of identity-principle based essentially on the contradistinction between *content* and *form*, that is 'between the message (as substance) and its medium (as style)' (Barthes 1984: 4). Nevertheless, this contradistinction has been challenged, indeed rendered obsolete, by semiotic analysis, and more particularly by concepts like intertextuality, stylistic plurality and connotation; and in the semiotics of the 'open' work of art, by aspects like temporality, the spatial dimension and references to different discourse genres, aspects that go well beyond the notion of style as indicative of formal and historical closure.

Barthes, moreover, detected a second contradistinction in the contemporary theoretical paradigm of style: the opposition between *norm* and *deviation*, which makes style an aberration (individual and institutional) from common usage (1984: 4). In virtue of this contradistinction, style would imply a moral vision: as an aberrant message, style 'surprises the code'; it is 'a difference, a distance' (1984: 6).

In challenging both these contradistinctions, Barthes sought a working hypotheses for 'considering stylistics features as transformations derived either from collective formulae ... or by a play of metaphor, from idiolectal forms' (1984: 9). Thus he proposes a kind of common model for style inspired by 'the conviction that style is essentially a citational process, a body of formulae, a memory (almost in the cybernetic sense of the word), a cultural and not an expressive inheritance' (1984: 9). It was from these reflections that Barthes developed his famous metaphor of discourse as being layered, like a pastry or an onion, rather than being like a fruit with a kernel (in which the flesh would be the form, or style, and the kernel, the content, or message) (1984: 10). A metaphor that we continue to use in the conviction that semiotics is an epistemology of the pastry or onion (depending on gastronomic taste) oriented towards: (1) a plurality of styles, (2) broadening the notion of style to cover a multiplicity of verbal and non-verbal discourses and sign systems (see Segre 1981: 562), (3) taking up the challenge of style as aberration.

I would like to extend what I call Barthes' 'common model' by following his suggestion of considering stylistic features as transformations that draw on, and enrich, that almost cybernetic memory rooted in culture. In this case, however, unlike the predominantly literary, or verbal, space within which Barthes moved, I would like to consider style as the production and effect of meaning in some non-verbal, or not-only-verbal, sign systems, to the extent that they participate in social discourses, and are themselves social discourses. In particular, this chapter will examine the stylistic features of some examples of body representation, features expressed in different languages through fashion, clothes, or a *look*.

In such contexts the notion of style is a familiar one, given the habit in the history of costume and fashion of speaking of dress styles, designer styles, or 'style' as synonymous with 'elegance'. In his analysis of forms and values, Omar Calabrese (following Woelfflin) writes that we may speak of, for example, a *baroque* style where we find formal openness, wit, double entendre and a variety of motifs, whereas we may speak of a *classical* style as one which 'independently of the figures through which it is expressed in any given historical moment, loves *disegno* and its formal precision, whole-ness, unity, perspectival depth and absolute intelligibility' (1992: 198). Calabrese speaks, moreover, of a 'cocktail effect' in fashion, whereby a blend of recognizable ingredients creates a new flavour which is more that just the sum total of the various parts (1992: 201–2).

The term 'worldliness' (see Perniola 1988 and Calefato 1992a, 1993, 1994) indicates the aspects of everyday life and social communication as well as the different discourses through which fashion is expressed: pho-tography, cinema, design, clothes, accessories, written descriptions of fashion and so on. In the context of worldliness it is impossible to give style a single definition and fashion itself becomes an open system for which a semiotic reading is possible, one that examines a whole range of trans-sty-listic features that cut across both the institutional and subcultural bound-aries of style. One of these trans- or metastylistic matrices is the grotesque: its characteristics of exaggeration, hyperbole, boundlessness, superabun-dance, semantic inversion, glorification of baseness, bodily openings and protuberances allow an exemplary analysis of the body's pluri-stylistic transformations, the perceptual decentring of objects and the exacerbation of received meaning (Bakhtin 1965).

Style has always been a key concept in the field of cultural studies, which considers bodily appearance styles as forms of aesthetic and ethical adher-ence to a culture-in-process filtered through dress, music, literature, cinema and daily routines. In his book *Subculture. The Meaning of Style* Dick Hebdige describes how in Jean Genet's *Diary of a Thief* an ordinary, everyday object, a tube of vaseline, sneered at by the policeman who con-fiscates it, becomes for the main character an emblem both of his 'crime' against the dominant sexual order and his triumph over it (1979: 1–3). In other words, it becomes a distinguishing feature of *style* as crime.

Typical of the styles defined by Hebdige as subcultural[1] is that they offer a paradoxical reading of everyday objects (like Genet's tube of vaseline or the Punk's safety pin) or of banal contrivances in one's appearance which are, nevertheless, painstaking in their details (like the Mod's dandy apparel), as a way of displaying one's codes, or at least of showing that the 'codes are there to be used and abused' (1979: 101). This operation is close to that of Surrealism: decontextualizing an everyday object and transposing it to an unusual or socially unacceptable place in order to highlight its status as sign. Hebdige compares this technique – for which he finds numerous examples in Punk – to those set forth in André Breton's Surrealist manifesto and to Lévi-Strauss' notion of *bricolage* (1979: 102–6).

In this sense styles would be social crimes, not so much in their explicit content or obviousness – it would be naive to think that body piercing and tattooing are transgressions in themselves – as in the fact that the ostentation of certain distinctive features 'denaturalizes' discourse, thereby revealing its semiotic status. Hebdige makes a distinction between style and fashion, seeing the latter as one of the 'prominent forms of discourse' (1979: 104). Here he is following Barthes' analysis of contemporary mythology as 'linguistic theft' (Barthes 1957: 212, 222 ff), the return of culture to nature in the form of *endoxa* (Barthes 1984: 1988: 65). Fifteen years after the publication of *Mythologies*, however, Barthes himself noted that there seemed to be a mythological *endoxa* which turned demystification (or demythification) itself into discourse (1984: 66). This tendency has greatly intensified in the last twenty years, during which time, even in the absence of an explicit semiology, the decodification of myth – the message in advertising, for example – has become more widely accessible, and the unnatural status of systems like the fashion system is even more apparent.

The distinction between the ideological status of subculture styles and that of fashion is no longer valid, however, since in the last 20 years the fashion system has knowingly become a sign in the eyes of its users. The presumed naturalness of expressions like 'prints win at the races' for the Barthesian reader of fashion magazines has been completely displaced by the widespread perception of fashion as discourse. Even the styles defined by Hebdige as subcultural have been absorbed by their opposite, institutionalized fashion. A Punk designer like Vivien Westwood, for example, is now the queen of British *haute couture*, and street styles have been transformed into what Ted Polhemus (1994) calls the 'supermarket of styles'.

With regard to the 'criminal' prerogative of style noted by Hebdige, rather than simply compiling an inventory of styles, it might be interesting to pursue paths of meaning, like the grotesque, along which style may be seen as a way of trimming off the excess in widespread semiotic material. The body is undoubtedly the main place where stylistic transformations take place; the body, that is, in the grotesque sense of 'clothed body', where covering is carnivalesque protuberance, parodic second skin, openness and not delimitation or boundary.

One of the distinctive features of the grotesque is hyperbolic enumeration, expressed through a conception of the body as a semiotic object – or subject – in process, in whose performances it is possible to invert the meaning of the different components, as well as the clothes and objects covering it.

An amusing example of this is the opening scene of *The Blues Brothers*, in which Jake (John Belushi) is released from prison and collects his personal belongings from the prison guard: a black hat, a pair of sunglasses, a new condom and a used one ... these details, typical of the attire of

Belushi and Aykroyd, are clues to the appearance style launched by the film, the meaning of which is conveyed through syntagmatic contiguity: the guard's list becomes a kind of proleptic inventory of the items that will go to make up a total *look*. Initially, however, it creates a feeling of suspense; indeed, until the guard has completed his list, Belushi has his back to the audience and we still have to wait through several more scenes before we see how this collection of items is arranged on his body.

The prolepsis continues with the arrival of Jake's brother, Elwood (Dan Aykroyd). The brothers dress exactly alike and even have the same names tattooed on their fingers. Aykroyd's outfit is an assemblage of the disparate items previously listed by the guard and anticipates Belushi's appearance from behind the prison gates, an appearance that now seems like a mystical apparition. Once donned, the pair's clothes and accessories are made up of the kind of assemblage that recalls a *bricolage*: the thread of meaning that connects these objects establishes a correspondence between clothed body and world order, not only within the film, but also in the relation of the film to its public. Every single item of clothing, particularly the sunglasses, becomes a fetish symbol and creates a vast and permanent uniform of tastes shared by several generations of young people who are fans of blues music and of the Blues Brothers.

From the opening scenes to the end of the film there is a sense of the strangeness of everyday objects and an excessiveness of gestures, which are made with marked self irony: the cigarette lighter Belushi throws out of the car window, the old 'bluesmobile' Aykroyd exchanges for a microphone, the police car used to pick up the ex-convict on parole, and so on.

There is an explicit reference to the Blues Brothers type in dark glasses in the film *Reservoir Dogs*, though here the director inverts the stylistic features of John Landis' film. Despite the fact that Jake and Elwood may at first seem like cruel ex-convicts, they turn out to be the good and affectionate former pupils of a group of nuns, whereas in the opening scene of *Reservoir Dogs* a group of criminals depicted in animated conversation over a banal and harmless topic soon live up to the violence implicit in the film's title. Another point of contrast is the space within which the action takes place: the claustrophobic atmosphere of *Reservoir Dogs* (most of the action is set in one large room) contrasts with the open space of *The Blues Brothers*, symbolically represented by the dance sequence that gradually spreads from Ray Charles' music shop to the sidewalk, the street and finally the whole neighbourhood, with more and more people joining in. This sequence contains a plurality, or polyphony, of styles, bodies, human types and ages that could well represent the diffusion of fashion in its worldly guise.

The opening scenes of Spike Lee's film *Malcolm X* depict the main character's initiation to the zoot style; another example of how a street style, which is aesthetic and existential at the same time, is assembled as a *bricolage* according to precise codes. The way of walking, the cut of the trousers, the long jackets and broad-brimmed hats, the bright colours and chemically straightened hair: everything is regulated by a standard, yet eccentric, code that made the zoot suit the distinctive sign of African-American male identity in the late 1930s and early 1940s, the public image of which was made famous by Cab Calloway.

The exaggerated fullness of the clothes and the flamboyant gestures, corresponding to a precise syntax described by Malcolm X in his autobiography, mark the zoot style as grotesque in the sense of hyperbolic, whereas artificially straightening the curly hair of African-Americans so that it looks like 'white' hair may be read as semantic inversion, whereby an appearance style overturns the socio-political hierarchy upheld by the antithesis white = positive, black = negative.

Polhemus' comments on the vicissitudes of the zoot suit in relation to wartime production are worth noting. He quotes an article in *The New Yorker* (1941) that suggests adopting a version of the zoot suit in mainstream male fashion, even though such suggestions could hardly have been taken seriously, when a few months later wartime regulations over fabric production drastically curtailed the use of wool, thus making it practically illegal, or in any case unpatriotic, to wear the eccentric and costly zoot suit, whose wide jackets and trousers required enormous amounts of fabric (Polhemus 1994: 18–19).

Polhemus also maintains that the zoot suit acted as a challenge to what the German psychologist Flugel has called 'the great male renunciation'; that is, the emergence of a male appearance style in the late eighteenth century corresponding to a sober and respectable identity, at the expense of experimentation and frivolity, which were relegated to women's fashion. The zoot suit thus represented a challenge that was all the more significant as a subcultural stratagem, since it came from the African-American community and coincided with the emergence of musical trends originating in the same community.[2]

Bakhtin writes that the grotesque is concerned 'with everything that bursts, protrudes and surfaces from the body, everything that seeks to escape the body's limits' (1965: 346–7). Punk is an interesting phenomenon, when seen from this perspective of the body's substantial limitlessness. For Punk, the body has no impenetrable surface, no insuperable limit: every inch of skin can be pierced by a safety pin, slashed by a blade or used for the exhibition of an unusual object, like a toilet chain or a sanitary towel. Hebdige highlights what could be called the Surrealist perspectival dislocation found, for example, in Vivien Westwood's 'confrontation dressing': if the hat doesn't suit you, then wear it, just as long as the gap between natural and artificial is clearly visible (Hebdige 1979: 107). Such a gap can be seen as part of the ironic prerogative of the grotesque: the moment one exhibits a contrast or an excess, one distances oneself from that very same exhibition. And herein lies the nihilistic potential of Punk, as well as its profound divergence from the politically committed anti-fashions of the 1960s and 1970s and back-to-nature hippie philosophy.

The importance of hairstyle in Punk is yet another display of 'grotesque' irony: a Mohican crest or Rasta deadlocks, elaborate headgear or totally artificial hair colour serve not only to create a dislocating and unnatural effect, but they also turn the body into the seat of self-referential signs that empty it of meaning. Another such example is dancing: according to Hebdige the pogo, the pose and the robot were all caricatures, a kind of *reductio ad absurdum* of rock music dance styles (1979: 108). And they too were forms of totally emptying the body: the pogo as self annihilation in the crowd, the pose and the robot as the transformation of human into automaton watching its own performance.[3]

In Pedro Almodovar's film *Kika* one of the female characters wears a leather dress and a camera on her head, a *look* created for the film by Jean Paul Gaultier, a designer familiar with this kind of experimentation in technological gear. As usual, fashion design is here inspired by styles and trends picked up in the street, amongst young people attracted by the avant-garde or aesthetically provocative. It is inspired by imaginary spaces, too, whether in literature or cinema, where appearance styles interpret, albeit in exaggerated form, our present condition of bodies covered by clothes *and* technology, from the digital watch to the mobile phone, from the electronic diary to the laptop computer.

In the late 1980s this condition led to a style commonly known as Techno, which became popular amongst rather restricted groups of young people, mainly in Europe and Japan, who flaunted an apocalyptic vision of the world and so chose to dress as if they were living through a science-fiction catastrophe (in anti-radiation suits, reflector sunglasses, urban commando camouflage and so on). Recently this style has spread in a tamer version and has been watered down to a more everyday *look*. So today it's not unusual to see 'normal' people dressed in transparent plastic coats, bags and shoes, or metallicized jackets and miniskirts.

Even *haute couture* has jumped on the bandwagon in the use of materials (the so-called 'new materials'), the cut of clothes and hairstyles. Yet in the absence of innovative designs, high fashion has just ended up regurgitating, at prohibitive costs, what was already on the street, in any case, or in science fiction novels and cult movies, like Wim Wenders' *To the End of the World*, set in a not-too-distant future in which wrist videophones and pocket computers are an integral part of the characters' appearance and communication styles.

In such a climate the step from Techno to its cousin Cyberpunk was a short one. The latter, however, is not based on apocalyptic visions, but takes its cue from the present state of technology and is inspired by the values of those who accept life in cyberspace and virtual reality as the true promise of transforming the world and human communication. On an aesthetic level, this style creates a *bricolage* out of industrial waste – rubber tubes, gas masks, etc. – and high-tech material – electronic circuits, holograms, robotic mechanical arms.

The prototype of Cyberpunk is to be found in novels such as William Gibson's *Neuromancer* (1984) in which the characters Cowboy Case and Molly are living examples of the interaction between the human and artificial-technological body. The rubber tubes of the fashion garment, for example, recall the wires that attach two electrodes to Case's temples, connecting him directly to the computer, where he lives in simulated places and has simulated experiences that, nevertheless, for him are completely real. The robotic arms, on the other hand, recall Molly's scalpel fingers, while the holograms are replicas of the characters' thoughts, which are able to produce three-dimensional images.

These fictional universes depict, whether in literary or cinematic form, our experiences in virtual reality today, with helmets, suits and sensors that simulate a whole range of bodily experiences.[4] In David Cronenberg's film *Videodrome* a man is transformed into a living video recorder: he can insert video cassettes into his body, which then act as though they were alive. In the short story 'Death of Reason' (1992) by the Cyberpunk writer Tony Daniel the main character wears 'op-ed' computer glasses that are activated simply by blinking.

Metallic accessories, coloured contact lenses, brooches and watches with holograms, studded belts (now almost a cliché), some with pseudo safety pins as a Punk reference, are all objects that reproduce in a tamer version the *look* of the characters in these narrative genres. Such technological styles, whether in their more eccentric manifestations or in the watered-down versions through which they influence fashion at all levels, reveal the extraordinary interaction between the various languages that now permeate our lives, especially the languages of dress and communications systems.

Cyberpunk culture is an expression of our 'wired' condition, perpetually part of a machine interface, or connected to a communications network that uses the human body as a support in a vaster 'nervous system' of cables, optic fibres and information technology in general. This condition is neither a paradox nor a literary gimmick, but a daily reality, whenever we use a mobile phone, credit card or electronic calculator, send a fax, an email or just go online. Nicholas Negroponte (1995) defines this phenomenon 'the transformation of atoms into bytes', that is, the transformation of matter into electronic impulses.

So style reveals its ethical dimension: whether Techno or Cyberpunk, doomster or virtual reality enthusiast, style shows us just how fast our way of communicating, moving and perceiving time and space is changing. With the added possibility of staging, so to speak, this reality, so that while we take it extremely seriously, we nevertheless criticize it, like the woman-camera in *Kika*, who is a parody of the journalist eternally in search of a photo scoop.

On a philosophical and cultural level, the wired dimension seems based on a vaster, more multifaceted sensibility than a subcultural aesthetic alone would suggest, as is shown by the work of Haraway (1991) and Perniola (1994), the former profoundly convinced of the validity of a cyborg ontology, the latter of the potential of Cyberpunk for philosophical productivity.

A semiotic analysis helps us identify the pluristylistic features of the genre: for example, in the description of a body in the short story 'Fool to Believe' (1990) by techno-feminist writer Pat Cadigan. The character's disguise (a policewoman hunting for criminals) is devised by an 'urban camouflage' computer program that makes it impossible to recognize her in the virtual slums. The transformation of her facial features has all the distinctive signs of a grotesque mask: cross-eyed, with idiotic eyebrows, a broken nose, punk-like hair and so on. The result is that she looks like an anonymous slum-dweller, yet for the reader her disguise has a surprisingly comic effect. Even the sound of the rasping voice and the 'gurgling over the aspirates' constitute grotesque features, just like the defects in pronunciation typical of comic masques. Indeed, this defective pronunciation issues from a body that seems to want to unburden itself, to give birth, so to speak, like the character who stutters in the *Commedia dell'Arte* and suffers from terrible labour pains in his attempts to pronounce a certain word, until Harlequin thumps him on the stomach and out pops the recalcitrant word, like a new-born babe.[5]

When a tension is set up between filling and emptying the body, the grotesque either maintains that tension or brings about its paradoxical resolution. In cyberspace, filling and emptying are not just a matter of atoms, of gorging and evacuating the body as in Rabelais, but also of bytes.

Caronia (1994) gives some interesting literary illustrations of this concept: in John Shirley's novel *Eclipse*, for example, dancers perform on stage attached to cables that let the music flow directly into their bodies and so they become 'wired' dancers.

In the old 007 films the hero is always supplied with a host of super-technological gadgets at the beginning of each new mission: ink pens, watches, shoes, briefcases, lighters and so on; common accessories that really hide a gun, rocket launcher, two-way radio, decoder and other fantastic devices that become increasingly sophisticated with each new film. Whoever, watching the early James Bond films from the 1960s, would have imagined that in the near future they themselves would have at their disposal an infinite variety of gadgets with the most disparate functions, perhaps not as deadly or camouflaged as those for Agent 007, but like them with the technology to empower human sensory and communicative faculties.

Even the most common remote control device (such as for our car or television) is just one of the many objects that are turning our bodies into an ensemble of technological prostheses. Indeed, we even adapt our habitual movements to these objects: in order to communicate with our car from a distance, for example, we have to change the position of our hands to digit a command, or we try and work out how far away we can be and still make it work, etc. And this is one of the most common techno-gadgets!

The most famous, of course, is the one that speaks for itself, the mobile phone, with which we are all familiar by now; and fortunately etiquette is spreading as to when, where, how and why we use it. If we look at the relation between body and object, every user seems to belong to a specific type: loud, discreet, ostentatious, embarrassed and so on. This mobile object has not only modified the possibilities and conditions of human communication, but has also brought about changes in the field of proxemics (the use human beings make of space) and kinesics (the meaning of our gestures).

And what about the typical behaviour of Walkman users, that portable object young people take everywhere? Isolated from the outside world, listening to their favourite CD, Walkman fans have become a symbol of contemporary urban life, the *flâneurs* of the twenty-first century. Indeed, Iain Chambers sees the Walkman as an object of modern nomadism and adduces the close relation between the micro-narratives introduced by the Walkman, which measures space musically, and the musical narratives of the aborigines described by Bruce Chatwin in *Songlines* (1987).[6]

Our pockets and handbags are increasingly filled with technological gadgets, such as the electronic pocketbook, which can even send and receive a fax, memorize names, phone numbers and appointments, and visualize them 'rationally' according to an order that effectively substitutes the 'disorder' of our traditional paper diaries. There is even an electronic pocketbook you can write in by hand, which then decodes your message.

We are all aware of the anthropological revolution brought about by objects like the laptop, which enable us to keep a travelogue or write home from the remotest corners of the globe, without having to bend over scraps of paper with a leaky pen. With a laptop at our disposal we can compose a potentially indestructible text with a few taps of the finger and email it anywhere. Another symbol of our slow transformation into cyborg is 'wrist technology', wristwatches that measure height, speed, depth, temperature, atmospheric pressure, latitude, longitude and even how many calories we are burning. Some wristwatches even function as electronic calculators, diaries and remote control devices. Technology thus recycles the same everyday object, but with a whole new range of extra functions.

The space that a semiotic conception of the grotesque opens up for a reading of the relation between different discourses is immense. Such an interrelation is based on the notion that there is mutual interpretation between discourses. Cinema, for instance, is not limited simply to bearing witness to new fashions, or to constructing a fashion world-stage, but reworks and recreates in exemplary and stylized form that which comes from the language of fashion, whether everyday or institutional. It even manages to represent shared tastes and sensibilities which are not yet fully articulated in everyday signs.

The grotesque image that perhaps best illustrates this interrelation is one of a mutual swallowing, like the Tarot card of the Wheel of Fortune, where it is impossible to distinguish one body from another. Just as the grotesque body can be depicted as a body swallowed by another body, swallowed by another and so on (Bakhtin1965: 347), so cross-discourse is a kind of swallowing of cultural fragments in the form of reference and citation. As Barthes writes, 'stylistic work is the search for models and patterns' (1984: 9). In other words, cultural fragments as repetition, reference, citation and stereotype. Yet as soon as grotesque stylistic features evince such models, they distance themselves with a kind of ironic pointing of the finger.

This is what happens when, in the intertexual commingling of different languages, body signs (from clothes to gesture) become the grotesque, yet completely serious, travesty of common social stereotypes. The dance scene in *Pulp Fiction* is a good example of this. In the exhilarating repetition of stereotypical dance movements and gestures, Mia and Vince's performance continues on the dance floor the clichés enacted by the living and inorganic replicas of 1950s and 1960s memorabilia. In another famous dance dialogue from a 1940s cartoon, Daffy Duck's jive with his partner, bodies and objects lose their 'normal' collocation and function (as always happens in cartoons, in any case) and a surreal scene is created in which all kinds of unpredictable and absurd events take place (like the popcorn popping in Daffy's stomach), while the stylistic model of the jive remains constant.

Citation as 'swallowing' has a fundamental role in fashion: its artifices are the techniques of revival and resemblance, together with the ostentation of details, poses and fetishes taken from contexts extrinsic to the fashion system. There are models by Martin Margiela, for instance, that seem artistic citations somewhere between the Surreal and the Metaphysical. On the catwalk, the hallmark of the designer's style is evident in the obliteration of the model's face. The mask is total and explicit: like the garment covering the body, the bag is a garment covering the face, that part of the body most exposed in western cultures. Dressing the body, including the face, disguising it hyperbolically, is thus an invitation to concentrate on the semiotic status of its impossible nakedness.

The film *Victor/Victoria* emphasizes another important aspect of grotesque 'swallowing' achieved through bodily disguise: sexual transvestism. Victoria, who is really a woman, pretends to be a man in drag who reveals his 'real' sex at the end of the show. The disconcerting effect of the burlesque and ironic triple transvestism is fully felt in the different reactions of the audience when Victor/Victoria comes on stage, both before and after the mock revelation that Victor is a man.

In a photo of Twiggy by Helmut Newton the model leaps up towards the ceiling in what seems to be a travesty of Batman, who appears on the TV screen below. The 'high' position of the body sets up a tension with regard to its imminent fall. This effect of 'waiting for the fall' classifies the photo as part of the 'outrageous' genre defined by Barthes as the most revolutionary of styles, since it substitutes 'its artifice, that is, its culture, for the false nature of things' (1967: 303). In *Empire of Signs* Barthes describes the movement of the body 'downwards' in the Japanese bow: 'Two bodies bow profoundly to one another ... according to a subtly codified hierarchy of depth' (1970: 77–8). Barthes speaks of an 'exercise of emptiness' connected to the body curving, sometimes even flattening itself, in this oriental gesture of courtesy, which he contrasts with the western gesture of 'fullness'. He calls the image 'Who is greeting whom?', thereby alluding to the fact that the bow suspends meaning, in what he calls the predominance of non-representative elements as an end in itself, not linked to the body as subjectivity (1970: 78).

The metastability of grotesque stylistic features lies in their inexhaustible potential for use in different semantic contexts. This metastability is narrated by Poe in the short story *The Man in the Crowd* in which a convalescent narrator amuses himself by scrutinizing the crowd's outward signs

– dress, hairstyle, gesture, gait and so on – and detecting in them the class, nationality, profession and character of each individual. In his deciphering he goes lower and lower in the scale of social values, from the businessman to the humble worker, from dusk to night, until he comes across the grotesque figure of a metropolitan demon, who so strikes him that he is compelled to follow him in a futile chase through the city streets. For the man in the crowd (here represented by the demon) will not let you read him; his mystery lies in the ambiguity of both standing out from and being part of the crowd from which he draws vitality and whose dispersion throws him into a state of agitation and confusion.

The stylistic features of the man in the crowd are masked by those of the myriad men and women in the street, to the extent that it becomes impossible for the narrator to continue his game, which was based on the conviction that style indicates a specific identity. Poe's short story is a theoretical goldmine, showing style as the result of the conflicting impulses of identification and dissimulation. And this is probably true for all the different manifestations of style – linguistic, literary, sociological and so on – which are situated at the crossroads between formal, aesthetic and ethical analysis.

Poe's man in the crowd has a direct descendent in Benjamin's *flâneur*, who is still visible in the street today in the form of youngsters with Walkmans on rollerblades (to use just one example). Contemporary figures, replicants in a world of stereotypes, are open to a semiotic reading of style as the transformation of these stereotypes until they explode as excess with regard to the world, while yet remaining profoundly *within* it.

Notes

1. Street styles from Teddy Boys and Mods to Skinheads and Punks.

2. A direct descendent of the Zoot style is the Hipster style created on the 1950s jazz scene by musicians like Thelonius Monk, Charlie Parker and Dizzy Gillespie.

3. This aspect of 'body-emptying' relates Punk to Cyberpunk and Techno styles in the 1980s and 1990s.

4. *Total Recall* and *Revelations* are two such films.

5. An example used by Bakhtin 1965.

6. In this book the author speaks of the Australian aborigines' belief that the earth was born from the songs of their ancestors.

4

Taste between Common Sense and Received Meaning

Baudelaire uses a familiar concept of worldliness when he speaks of Constantin Guys as 'the painter of modern life' and emphasizes his being 'a man of the world, or better, a man of the whole world, someone who comprehends the world and the mysterious, legitimate reasons for all its ways.' Guys is someone who does not want to be alone in his art, but who seeks 'to know, understand and evaluate everything that happens on the surface of our planet' (Baudelaire 1863: 283). For Baudelaire, Guys is more of a dandy than an artist in that he has 'a quintessence of the character [of the dandy] and a subtle awareness of the moral mechanisms of the world' (285). Moreover, Guys is decidedly removed from the tendency to insensibility and he is thus a man of the world dominated by 'an insatiable desire to hear and to see'. This artist's domain is the crowd: 'being part of the crowd is his passion and profession', even though the crowd is 'a human desert' (288) whose general approval does not correspond to his aspirations.

Guys' sketches depict scenes from everyday life and news items: the Crimean War is illustrated through portraits of soldiers, life on the boulevards through images of the dandy, prostitutes, elegant carriages and 'everyday' fashions. Guys sees modernity as all that is 'transitory, fleeting, contingent; half of art, the other half being the eternal and immutable.' And so he distils from fashion (from the stuff of everyday life) 'what it contains of the poetic and extracts the eternal from the ephemeral' (Baudelaire 1863: 288).

In his reflections on Paris as the capital of the nineteenth century, Walter Benjamin writes that what particularly fascinated Baudelaire about Guys was his 'background technique', through which he could present things to the gaze as if they were close up, yet in such a way that the eye could still measure the magnitude of the distance, like the gaze of the oriental prostitute drawn by the same painter. In this detail and in Baudelaire's assessment of Guys as a worldly painter, Benjamin gleans a parallel with his notion of the reproducible work of art that has lost its aura, its spell-binding 'far-off gaze' (1982: 402–3). Benjamin also sees a close resemblance between Baudelaire's depiction of Guys and Nietzsche's 'Indian pessimism' with its 'unexpected, nostalgic, fixed expression in which the void is reflected.' In the gaze of the oriental prostitute turned towards the horizon 'the most fixed attention and the most profound disorientation' converge (1982: 482).

Benjamin grasps the extraordinary intuition of Baudelaire's conception of the metropolis: he is the first writer to describe Paris by 'evoking the sea of houses with its gigantic waves', unlike the more primitive Balzac, whose characters 'are larger than the streets through which they move' (1982: 31a). With its crowded streets and artificially illuminated nights, Paris is where the definitive crisis of the Kantian sublime takes place. An expression like 'the moral law within me, the starry sky above me' is unimaginable for a denizen of the metropolis, where artificial lighting has obliterated the stars (1982: 444–5).

The world that populates the modern metropolis is the crowd, a veil that hides the masses, a simulacrum of individuals (Benjamin 1982: 432), yet where each individual has an unmistakable physiognomy, like Poe's man of the crowd, the inspiration for Baudelaire's notion of worldliness (1982: 430).

For Benjamin, the crowd is illusory duplication, part of the phenomenon of fetishism, as described by Marx in relation to his notion of alienation. In his 1844 manuscripts Marx describes how, in alienated work, an object, the product of the worker's efforts, looms before its maker like an 'alienated thing' or an 'independent force'. Work has become objectified and this fact turns not only the products of labour (that is, merchandise), but also the work and the worker into *things* (Marx 1844: 194–5). The universality of humankind, as *Gattungswesen*, manifests itself in the relation between humankind and nature (1844: 198). Work deprives the human being of both nature and gender: nature becomes alienated and the body is appropriated, becoming a shell, an inorganic support. Social nature, too, becomes a *thing* and thus functions independently of the human being, from which it is separated. Fetishism represents the moment of perverse glorification of this *thing*.

Baudelaire's world, writes Benjamin, has collapsed into the cadaverous rigidity of fashion and prostitution (1982: 430). In the modern metropolis prostitution has become a metaphor for money and work; its mercenary character increases its allure, as does the fact that the metropolitan multitudes allow a sex object to be reflected simultaneously in hundreds of different forms of seduction (1982: 439, 451). Fashion, on the other hand, is the sex appeal of the inorganic, the sex appeal of devitalized nature, of the corpse-like body as merchandise (1982: 70, 124–6). In the form of merchandise, the *thing* produces an effect of alienation between human beings, since the price of merchandise, its hard cash equivalent, is completely indifferent to the work that has produced it and the human qualities of such work are transformed into the only value admissible in the capitalist metropolis, that of equal exchange (1982: 505).

There is a close affinity between prostitution and fashion, based on a notion of the world as a great exchange market, a simulacrum of human relations, where nature itself assumes the character of merchandise (Benjamin 1982: 447). In the form of prostitution found in the worldly metropolis, writes Benjamin, woman appears not only as merchandise, but as a mass-produced item. Modern prostitution is thus characterized by serial repetition, analogous to the reproducibility of merchandise. An example of this is the standardized and professional function of the prostitute's makeup or the show-girl's costume (1982: 449).

Baudelaire sees in the metropolitan figure of the prostitute a 'multifarious image of equivocal beauty' (1863: 309). And he describes how 'women have exaggerated fashion to the point of despoiling its grace and destroying its aim.' The prostitute belongs to the type of wayward and rebellious woman found in every social class, whom one meets in 'that immense gallery of [metropolitan] life' (1863: 310). Baudelaire's image of the prostitute depicts woman as both a figure of discourse and a challenge to the order of discourse; as both representation and the object of representation, on the one hand, and as an historical being, a relational subject, on the other (see Calefato 1994: 59). The play of clothing, of covering, in other words, the bodyscape, is essential to this ambivalence.

Starting from the metaphysical definition of allegory as the 'semblance of freedom, independence and infinity' (1982: 419) Benjamin places whole collections of Baudelaire's poetry in this allegorical scheme, from *Les Fleurs du Mal* to *Révolte* and *Spleen et Idéal*. For Benjamin allegory represents 'what merchandise has transformed human experience into this century' (1982: 422). Existence is seen as wreckage and fragmentation: for example, Baudelaire's 'fragmented' descriptions of the female body, or his image of the body as fetish, as a body-thing ('Statue aux yeux de jais, grand ange au front d'airain' (1982: 425). In the allegorical scheme noted by Benjamin, however, there is an implicit dialectic: the 'destructive fury' of allegory tends to obliterate the wreckage in a 'regressive tendency', yet it also tends to eliminate the 'illusory appearance that emanates from a given order, whether in art or life … so that such an order becomes bearable' and herein lies its 'progressive tendency' (1982: 427).

Finally, in the relation between these two writers, a concept of the world emerges that has the same ambivalence as allegory. The modern world is, indeed, a world of appearances, of the mystic veil, simulacra, ruins, corpses and the inorganic, but it is also a world that can transcend its own illusory nature (as a given order). Fashion is a system of exchange between the world and merchandise; it is 'a means of transferring the character of merchandise to the cosmos' (1982: 70). Its status makes it similar to Benjamin's 'figure of passage' (see Calefato 1992a). Moreover, fashion exhibits the sex-appeal of merchandise, of the inorganic, in a paradoxical game, a parodic inversion that does indeed make the lifeless fascinating and seductive, and where the *thing* replaces the person.

The sex appeal of the inorganic – that is, the allegorical dimension of fashion in the modern metropolis – doesn't only have a negative value. On the contrary, fashion is invigorated by the very duplicity of its forms of seduction, crystallized in stereotypes and commonplaces, on the one hand, yet overturning these very same stereotypes in a carnivalesque rendering of bodily forms, on the other.

Benjamin's reflections on fashion in the modern age, inspired by Baudelaire's writings and by a constant analysis of the material forms of the nineteenth century metropolis, lay the grounds for understanding the transformations, discerned by Simmel at the end of the nineteenth century, that have taken place in fashion in terms of its 'classical' status. In Simmel's analysis of the status of fashion in modernity, fashion objectifies and equalizes opposing currents: imitation and innovation, internal and external, individual and society (1895: 61). Simmel's concept of objectification expresses the prerogative of fashion to make manifest, to promote to collective image, the dialectic between individual and society, providing the latter with a third horizon of representation that does not invade the individual's spiritual territory.

In looking at the revival of the classical status of fashion from a fresh perspective, Benjamin nevertheless feels that this objectification has become fetishism, that the mediation between the two tensions (individual and social) adumbrated by Simmel has turned them into lifeless forms and fashion into the parody of a decaying corpse (Benjamin 1982). Even the concept of 'passage' in reference to the cityscape of Paris as the nineteenth century capital, epitome of the modern metropolis, only becomes valid when individual memory and experience have been 'massified' and spread through the crowd. For Benjamin, 'revival' consists in making the dialectic an up-to-date one, from a perspective of alienation implicit in the modern division of labour, as well as in the automatism regulating how the urban masses behave. Here alienation extends to intellectual, dream and sign work in general, and to the processes of alienation identified by Marx in the production of merchandise. Such an extension also defines the field of communication as the production, consumption and exchange of verbal and non-verbal signs (Rossi-Landi 1985: 27–45).

Today communication defines the boundaries of the world. Indeed, Benjamin's reflections shed light on our present notion of communication, since they clearly and concisely define modern forms of communication as worldliness, as *mass* communication. Fashion is one of these forms, yet the very term 'fashion' is today ambiguous (as indeed it was for Benjamin). On the one hand, it is institutional, spectacular and consumer-oriented – *haute couture*, the catwalk, the top model – while, on the other, it is eccentric and linked to alternative forms of culture and incipient ideologies – street styles and anti-fashions (see Perniola 1988, Calefato 1992a, 1994). Today these two aspects are increasingly separate: the institutional side tends to be conventional and ideologically conservative, while fashion in its worldly guise is more unconventional and widespread.

Yet worldliness has always been a part of fashion, in that following a fashion has always meant expressing a relation to the world. Today, however, the relation between the individual and the world as expressed through fashion is *total*, since fashion has invaded the whole territory of the human spirit. Putting on clothes means following the imaginary laws of dress and circulating the body, in a sort of law of resemblances that produces an image of dress as a vessel of otherness. In *Fragments of a Lover's Discourse*, Barthes, quoting Goethe in *The Sorrows of Young Werther*, writes that clothing is the shell, or involucrum, of the image, in this case the amorous image (1977: 15). Like Werther, Barthes writes, 'I long to be the other and for the other to be me through my amorous clothes' (see Calefato 1986, 1992a). Dress is where the identity of one's own body becomes confused; worldliness is the dimension within which clothing, imagery, a style and a *look* go beyond fashion, while still retaining some of its features.

Through the masks of worldliness, today the clothed body is more than just an automaton, more than just a body in the age of technical reproduction. It has become a mutant body, a body that changes its appearance in virtue of relational values and a category of otherness implicit in the term 'worldly'. These values produce lifestyles that lead to aesthetic choices, patterns of behaviour, aspirations and projects which otherwise would not be 'with the times' except in the most conventional sense.

Fashion may be considered as a socio-semiotic mediation between taste and received meaning, or *common sense* (in Latin *sensus communis*, see below). My starting point here is Kant's *Critique of Judgement*, in which taste is taken to mean *common sense*. In 1970 Hannah Arendt gave a series of lectures on Kant in which she formulated a political interpretation of the *Critique of Judgement* and linked the notion of *common sense* to that of community. She reminds us that until 1787 the work was called *Critique of Taste*, and indeed taste is central to the whole work, which, even though not overtly political, picks up on the revolutionary climate in Europe after the French and American Revolutions, a climate in which critical thought had political implications (Arendt 1982: 61). 'Thinking critically,' she writes, 'carving out a path between unfounded prejudices, opinions or convictions, is an age-old concern of philosophy' (59). Kant himself was obviously well aware of the origin of philosophy in critical thought, and Arendt believes that he extended this philosophical prerogative to the public, communicative sphere (69).

In Arendt's reading of Kant the relation between taste and *common sense* is actuated through language as public communicability. The communicability of taste lies not in the *content* of a judgement, but in the *form* of a representation; in other words, it is a *condition* of the possibility of representation itself. Arendt here plays with the meaning of the word 'taste' as related to the five senses, and argues that while sight, touch and hearing perceive things in a direct and 'objective' way, smell and taste convey internal sensations which are difficult to communicate (1952: 98).

So how is it, Arendt asks, that the sense of taste – starting with Graciàn, but above all in Kant – has been elevated to the spiritual faculty of judgement? The answer is to be found in the fact that taste, like the palate, gives free reign to the imagination, to the faculty of 'making present what is absent', an operation defined by Kant as 'reflection' (1982: 99). And imagination is only possible through inter-subjectivity: 'one has to be alone in order to think, but one needs to be in company to enjoy [*sic*: taste] a meal' (Barthes 1975 xxxix).

The 'dialogue' between Arendt and Kant is particularly interesting from a semiotic perspective. Imagination, as the faculty of making present what is absent, which is triggered by *common sense*, indicates the possibility of something functioning as a sign: semiosis, sign-work. Taste as physical sensation is described by Barthes, in his reading of Brillat-Savarin, in terms of the relation between taste and language:

> Brillat-Savarin speaks, and I desire the things he speaks of (especially if I'm hungry). Since the desire stimulated by the gastronomic utterance is apparently simple, the utterance presents the power of language in all its ambiguity: the sign evokes the delights of its referent the very moment in which it charts their absence. (Barthes 1978: xxxix)

Arendt's political reading of the relation between taste and *sensus communis* in Kant may be likened to Gramsci's concept of *common sense* as 'spontaneous philosophy' – a readily accessible sense of things devoid of metaphysical abstruseness – and 'good sense', evidence of which may be traced to language, popular religion and that system of beliefs and opinions commonly called 'folklore' (Kant 1790 §40; It. tr. 151). Yet Gramsci also took account of *common sense* as stereotyped, generic, automatic thought and speech, and as prejudice. In order to demonstrate the difference between good sense and *common sense* he used a passage in *I promessi sposi* about the plague and the fact that the few who refused to believe the plague-spreaders' story could not defend their opinion against the more general popular one: 'Good sense was there,' writes Manzoni, 'but it was hidden by the fear of common sense' (Gramsci 1975: 1483).

Kant, on the other hand, felt that this duplicity could be avoided by practising his three maxims of *common sense*: (1) think for yourself; (2) think by putting yourself in someone else's place; (3) think in such a way as to be always in agreement with yourself (Arendt 1982: 68–9, 95). Kant felt that the negation of the first maxim (not thinking for yourself) generated prejudice, the opposite of enlightenment. *Common sense* can never be prejudice, since it contains within itself a way of thinking which is free, extensive and coherent, qualities corresponding respectively to the three maxims.

Not accepting passively the point of view of others, but testing it against the first and second maxims is what broadens the mind, expands and extends thought. Arendt glimpsed the political nature of Kant's philosophy (and, we might add, of the concept of taste itself) in this notion of community. An important quality semiotically, too, since the subject in this community is the 'world spectator', *Weltbetrachter*, on which meaning, as 'the observer's judgement', is based (Arendt 1982: 98). The condition for such a judgement, which produces disinterested pleasure, is taste. Kant notes that the loss of this *sensus communis* permitting us to judge as spectators leads to folly, as the ostentation of *sensus privatus*. Thus in the Kantian system there is a direct link between taste and reason.

Arendt interprets the difference between the English *common sense* (in German *Gemeinsinn*) and the Latin *sensus communis*, or *community sense* (in German *Gemeinschaftlicher Sinn*), as the difference between 'the same sense for everyone in private' (*common sense*) and an 'extra sense' that places us in a community (*community sense*), and through which the authentic humanity of each individual manifests itself (1982: 108). For Arendt, the fact that *sensus communis* is a specifically human attribute is closely connected to the fact that it depends on communication, on language as the true dimension of human community. Implicit in this community dimension is a very particular form of persuasion, one that takes account of the fact that even if you cannot persuade anyone to agree with your judgements on taste, you can nevertheless appeal, through language, to a *community sense* where taste loses its idiosyncratic nature (111–12).

Fashion may be considered as a system capable of guaranteeing a mediation between taste, *common sense* and community.[2] It represents the sign system through which the communication of taste, in the Kantian form of 'the activity of reflection',[3] is fully realized. Fashion is immediate communicability and the formulation of taste irrespective of the contents of taste itself. Moreover, fashion concerns a condition of taste that may be defined tautologically: the value of fashion, as dictated by taste, is measured simply in terms of 'being fashionable', without any functional, objective or practical reference.

Conceiving of fashion as a sign system means considering it in relation not only to its signification, but also to its significance. Fashion is based on value-situations in which individuals behave according to preferences. And a value-situation is, by definition, relational, since the values that enter into play in human behaviour are never wholly objective, nor wholly subjective. A condition of aesthetic value-situations is certainly taste, which in the Kantian sense of *sensus communis* extends aesthetic value to include community choices and behaviour; that is, taste forges a link between aesthetics and politics, as Arendt gleaned in the *Critique of Judgement*.

The concept of value is determined by 'value-making human behaviour', according to Rossi-Landi; that is, by 'the human ability to produce values and live them'. Often the analysis of value-situations takes slight account of the role of language. This leads us to think habitually of values as adjectives organized around pairs: 'good-bad', 'ugly-beautiful', 'just-unjust' and so on; or of nouns which are by nature neither positive nor negative (Rossi-Landi 1954: 34). In reality, Rossi-Landi maintains, the noun already contains within itself a positive or negative value, and this becomes clear when we think of nouns like 'state', 'community' and 'individual', which are 'already invested with a value-type, either positive or negative'.

Rossi-Landi excludes two positions from the attribution of values: *objectivism*, in which values are inherent to the structure of things external to human beings, and *subjectivism*, in which values are inherent to the structure of the evaluating 'I' (1954: 35). Rossi-Landi contrasts 'value-making human behaviour' to both these ontological positions that presume semiotic material to be organized according to values independently of the processes and modes of the production of values. To the question 'what happens when we speak of value?' Rossi-Landi replies by proposing to examine the concept of value without reducing the problem to an empirical level of usages, techniques or inventories, but by examining value 'at the source', so to speak, as a model of human behaviour; an examination of the conditions necessary for the possibility and the ways of making values.

This concept of value is far from the market research definition of value, based on the analysis of trends, opinion polls, statistics and all that concerns values as produced in their empirical reality. There is a difference between fashions and trends, especially if we consider fashion as worldliness; that is, in relation to non-institutional values. The value of a trend is implicit in utterances that often reflect prejudices, commonplaces and received meanings. The value of fashion, on the other hand, is one that represents itself and nothing else; a commonplace, if you like, but in the rhetorical sense of *locus communis*, a 'meeting place' in language and taste. In this context the Kantian *a priori* method grasps the self-referential nature of fashion values, even though today it is important to translate the Kantian 'conditions of possibility' into a socio-semiotic method.

I alluded above to the importance Arendt attributes to Kant's 'world spectator', the denizen of a cosmopolitan community, where meaning is generated as 'the observer's judgement'. In a certain sense, fashion is antecedent to this judgement, for which it sets up the conditions by orienting taste. If the Kantian relation between taste and judgement may be schematized as follows:

taste – imagination – reflection – *sensus communis* – judgement

then we may hypothesize that fashion is placed somewhere in the middle of this trajectory. Meaning is 'the observer's judgement' to the extent that this 'observer' may be taken as a semiotic subject-in-process created along this trajectory, and not as a given.

In reading Kant, Arendt notes that for him the opposite of beauty isn't ugliness, but anything that arouses disgust (1982: 104). Indeed, taste can produce judgements of aesthetic value even for what is considered 'ugly' in nature (Kant 1970 §48; It. tr.: 171).

Kant's notion of disgust may be related to the quasi-psychological mechanism identified by Benjamin, who writes that every generation sees the fashion of the previous generation as 'the most potent anti-aphrodisiac that one can imagine' (1982: 124). For Benjamin the general feeling of disgust for yesterday's fashions reflects a judgement which captures a salient feature of fashion, that of containing 'a bitterly satirical attitude to love' and 'the most shameless perversions'. And it is this perversion that unleashes either the paradoxically devitalized and cadaverous sex-appeal of fashion, or its opposite, disgust and total loss of attraction for yesterday's fashions.

Benjamin grasps, in exemplary manner, what he calls 'the dialectical performance' of fashion, its capacity to make the latest novelty catch on, but only when it emerges in the midst of the old, the habitual and the 'has-been' (1982: 106). While fashion is the search for the new, it has to formulate this 'new' in a tame version that appears familiar. In reality, fashion is able to formulate this dialectic because it moves between taste and *common sense*; thus, the ugly, kitsch, bizarre and parodic can gain approval or, at least, social acceptance given the peculiar mechanisms of how fashion functions, not only in its baroque, but also in its pop and worldly guises.[4] Especially in its worldly guise, fashion has managed to orient taste towards *common sense*, even when certain styles or attitudes haven't managed to gain general approval (pop styles, for example), but have been judged as being in bad taste. High fashion has absorbed elements from Punk, for example, and in everyday dress today, objects and clothing practices which might at first seem exotic or eccentric are generally accepted and shared.

Hans Magnus Enzensberger, in an interview in the Italian newspaper *La Stampa*, set out a kind of manifesto against the ugly in fashion, in which he complained about the fact that the dictatorship of classical fashion was over; it had made us attentive to trends, models and styles in the reassuring certainty that they would all quickly disappear. For Enzensberger this dictatorship of fashion as 'beauty' and 'equilibrium' has gone forever and what is left is 'the ugly', which he has defined as the perennial masquerade of the human body as a 'shapeless salami', where 'what you are must be totally denied' (Enzensberger 1993).

With a moralism that would be unthinkable if practised in the name of fashion, which is itself amoral, Enzensberger expatiates on disgusted descriptions of how today the clerk at the post office prefers to look like someone who vandalizes slot-machines and the high-school students comes to the exams looking like Rambo, while an illiterate person wears a T-shirt with 'University of Southern California' written on it. What the writer is complaining about is the loss of identity celebrated by contemporary fashions, to the point that the only people who have remained 'themselves' are those who are faithful to 'a wardrobe adequate to their role in life, whether it be that of a waiter or a minister, a baker or a general'. Enzensberger's invective against this 'rubbish' follows in the tradition of detractors of fashion in every age, who have found it culpable on two different counts:

1 For one school of criticism, any aesthetic preoccupation with adorning and painting the body distances human beings from nature and its precepts, whether earthly or divine. For example, at the beginning of the third century Tertullian, in *De cultu feminarum*, inveighed against the diabolical origins of the art of makeup and of ornament in dress, defining the clothes and beauty care of those who practised the 'cult' (i.e. women) as 'wanton acts of prostitution'.

2. For the other school, fashion is to be condemned as a mirror of the times, since the times it mirrors are to be condemned. For example, in 1827 Leopardi ironically compared fashion to death, since both were the children of Transience, and defined his age not only the 'century of fashion', but also the 'century of death'.

The ingenuous belief in the naturalness of beauty was stigmatized once and for all by Baudelaire in *Eloge du maquillage*. In the modern age, especially the twentieth century, the enemies of fashion have mainly adopted a sardonic attitude towards modernity as decadence. Adolf Loos spoke of the 'degenerative character' of ornament and defined women's fashion as 'an atrocious chapter in the history of civilization', while Walter Benjamin's 'sex-appeal of the inorganic' celebrated by fashion both fascinated and repelled. Enzensberger's refrain apes the style of a Benjamin or a Loos without their gift for not taking themselves too seriously.

The anti-fashion of the 1960s and 1970s targeted 'bourgeois' fashion as status symbol, yet ended up promoting a fashion of its own. The enemies of fashion in the 1980s (the decade of its almost metaphysical celebration), like Jean Baudrillard, saw in it 'the phantasmagoria of the code', that is, the ultimate, symbolic expression of fashion as merchandise. Gilles Lipovetsky saw fashion as representing 'the empire of the ephemeral', while Ugo Volli (1988) proposed to counter this with a 'semiotic ecology' that would decontaminate the world of the excess of messages which, like fashion, were able to prevail only in virtue of their capacity for self-destruction. Enzensberger lamented the death of fashion in the name of an alleged identity that, in his opinion, was still possible in classical fashion. For the German writer, the ugly is represented, for example, by wide, short, dirty trousers, leather jackets and jeans. But who decides what is ugly anyway? Who is to judge? The semiotic subject judges according to the popular saying 'It's beautiful because I like it' and what we like can be called fashionable. It is what we talk about as shared taste; it is taste as chatter; it is what circulates with street credibility.

Against Enzensberger were all those designers, like Fiorucci and Dolce & Gabbana, who saw in contemporary fashion (particularly their own) a sort of worldly version of the artistic avant-garde whose excesses, eccentricities and chaotic nature they therefore strenuously defended. Advocates of classical fashion, on the other hand, came out in support of the writer's views. Giorgio Armani maintained that since the 1980s his style had been aimed at counterbalancing the grotesque and the confusion of identities and personalities in fashion. One has the impression that Enzensberger's main target is street fashion, which is in any case free from the obligations and dictates of high fashion, and yet is governed by its own rhetorical codes. This fashion, contaminated by the ugly and by 'rubbish', with the grotesque and camouflage as its prerogatives, is light years away from any totalitarian aesthetic practice which eliminates from its field of influence all that is unacceptable, excessive or eccentric in human existence. The fashion whose demise Enzensberger lamented is institutional fashion, the confirmation of identity, and the denial of anything that in a perfect, closed body escapes its bounds. Unlike this fashion regime, street styles can still give us bursts of carnivalesque fun, which is, in effect, the derision of totalitarianism in all its forms.

In Ernst Lubitsch's film *Ninotschka*, the heroine (Greta Garbo), newly arrived in Paris as a government official from the Soviet Union, comments on a fashionable hat in a shop window: 'A civilization with such horrible tastes is bound to disappear.' Yet Ninotschka goes back later to look at that hat with a growing curiosity, and in the end we see it on her head, symbolically sanctioning the grey and serious commissar's rite of passage to western fashion. The metaphor in the film expresses, in this case, the oscillations, aberrations, as well the speed with which tastes spread and come to be shared.

The worldly mechanisms of fashion include forms of taste in tension; contradictory and provocative forms that can spread in leaps and bounds, with interruptions and unexpected returns, local explosions, counter citations and so on. This socio-semiotic mechanism is quite different from the one highlighted in Simmel's socio-psychological analysis of fashion in 1895, which nevertheless foresaw the contrast between diffusion and transience as one of the driving forces of the fascination exercised by fashion. The movement indicated by Simmel concerned the famous 'dripping' effect of fashion in an age when the latter was still not a means of mass communication. Indeed, the tension, the chaotic and contradictory nature of taste in fashion are all characteristics linked to its 'mass' aspect, which only fully came into being at the end of the 1950s. The expression 'oscillations in taste' coined by Dorfles at the end of the 1960s refers to the mass media dimension of the arts, including fashion, a dimension for which the Italian scholar identified precursory signs as far back as Art Nouveau.

We can now certainly speak of a chaotic mechanism in the communication of taste through fashion-as-worldliness: the slightest change, the most absurd invention produced at any point in the global communications systems, can be amplified enormously and spread at lightning speed over vast distances.

This mechanism in the diffusion of contemporary fashion has been called the 'trickle-up' (Ash-Wilson 1993) or 'bubble-up' (Polhemus 1994) effect, indicating a movement bottom-top, or down-up, contrary to the traditional movement up-down ('trickle-down') from high to street fashion, from élite social groups to the lower échelons. The notion of chaos, however, goes beyond the verticality of expressions such as these, used to indicate how fashion spreads, because it expresses the oscillation and sharing of tastes in a communicative sphere where *common sense* is formed on both a global and a local level, in both centres and peripheries.

Lotman (1993) describes the relation between the predictable and the unpredictable as the tension between two opposing variables in the movement of cultural signs. He also deals with the theme of fashion under two headings: dandyism and the topsy-turvy. The first appears in reference to a dialogue in Bulwer-Lytton's novel *Pelham* between a real dandy and an imitator (Lotman 1993: 19). The contenders discuss the kind of relationship that should exist between a man and his tailor: 'Give me a man who creates his tailor, not the tailor his man', says the dandy, thus summing up a maxim of dandyism which is absolutely inapplicable to fashion as imitation, yet perfectly in line with its innovative element. For Lotman, the confrontation between dandy and imitator highlights the problem of the relation between an 'authentic explosion' (here represented by the creative, aesthetic and ethical values of the dandy, which are only so for him, however) and an 'imitation explosion', the vulgar aping of dandyism, which nevertheless in the public eye passes for the real thing, while for Lotman it is a form of 'anti-explosion'.

So fashion contains two opposing tensions: Lotman explains and expands this paradox by placing fashion within the dynamics of a topsy-turvy world. Fashion 'introduces a dynamic principle in seemingly immobile everyday spheres' (1993: 103). These everyday spheres, which traditional costume tends to maintain unchanged through time, are invaded by fashion. Fashion manages to release into the everyday those antithetical characteristics with which it is normally associated: it is capricious, voluble, arbitrary and unmotivated.

'Fashion is always semiotic,' writes Lotman (1993: 104) and, he continues, this manifests itself particularly in the fact that 'it always implies an observer'. Here again is the political and semiotic question raised by

Arendt in her reading of Kant, of taste linked to the observer's judgement. Lotman admits, however, that he is unable to find a resolution for the duality élite/mass in fashion, and thus he concludes that without, or beyond, shocking the public, fashion loses its meaning. Freely interpreting Lotman, the observer's judgement would cause a constant explosion, ferment and excessiveness in taste, whereas we know that, in spite of everything, fashion can also be calming for the subject, and this characteristic manifests itself in the mediation between individual taste and *common sense* which fashion guarantees. How does this happen? How is this mediation possible? The topsy-turvy process noted by Lotman surely plays an important role here. Bakhtin, as we have seen, sums this up in the image of the grotesque body's semantic inversion.

Carnivalesque inversion is possible through the worldly modes of fashion. The clothed body is grotesque; it is a semiotic category expressing the way in which the subject is in the world, through his/her appearance style, his/her relation to other bodies and to his/her own bodily experiences. Moreover, the concept of the clothed body implies that a spectator interferes with the image of the closed, ascetic body. This spectator must be 'other' than the body, though not as its disinterested or distant analyst, but profoundly *within* it. The young heroine of *L'amant* expresses this well when, speaking of her hat, she says: 'I saw myself as another, as another would be seen, from the outside, there for everyone, for everyone's gaze, let loose in the flux of cities, streets, and pleasures' (Duras 1984: 18). This seeing oneself as another, and as another would be seen, is for the heroine a source of sensuous pleasure, linked to tasting, to savouring a new experience. The clothed body savours itself as if it were savoured by others, as if this tasting were the movement itself, the common, public circulation of sense.

Notes

1. Translator's note: *common sense* as used by Kant, and subsequently Arendt, to indicate a general consensus of meaning.

2. Both in the narrow sense and the Kantian cosmopolitan sense.

3. The critical sharing of the conditions of the possibility of representation.

4. Pop style indicates the inclusion in élite cultural contexts of subcultural styles and traits coming from restricted groups; see Wark 1992: 152–4. Worldly modes indicate the forms in which these subcultural traits, together with 'baroque' experimentation, are included in a traditionally 'classical' context of everyday clothing and body aesthetics; see Calefato 1992a, 1993, 1994.

5

Everyday Models

In *The Fashion System* Barthes writes:

> ... the cover girl represents a rare paradox: on the one hand, her body has the value of an abstract institution, and on the other, this body is individual; and between these two conditions, which correspond exactly to the opposition between Language and Speech, there is no *drift* ... this structural paradox defines the cover girl utterly: her essential function is not aesthetic, it is not a question of delivering a beautiful body, subject to the canonic rules of plastic success, but a deformed body, with a view to achieving a certain formal generality, i.e., a structure. It follows that the cover girl's body is no one's body, it is a pure form, which possesses no attribute ... and by a sort of tautology, it refers to the garment itself; here the garment is not responsible for signifying a full, slim, or slight body, but, through this absolute body, for signifying itself in its own generality ... (1967: 258–9)

Barthes' cover girl is the paper model, the written woman of described fashion, the 'ideal incarnate body ' in fashion imagery. In the cover girl's body Barthes identifies a structural paradox: it is both an abstract and an individual body. The aesthetic canon of the 'beautiful body' is supplanted by a deformation aimed at generality and dispossession, whereby the body signifies the garment; not a specific garment, however, but a general class of signifieds, all related to the main signified, which for Barthes is 'being-in-fashion'. This takes place within a fashion system made up of glossy pages, and of users who are mainly readers; in other words, a communication system almost entirely based on writing and literalness, the cohesion of signifier and signified, as in the system of described fashion in the 1950s and 1960s analysed by Barthes.

These were crucial years for the transformation of fashion into a 'total' means of mass communication, no longer reliant on other forms of communication, such as specialized magazines, but a space in itself for the production and reproduction of meaning. Barthes intuitively sensed this in speaking of a 'rhetorical system' that could be added to the structure of signifier and signified, and in speaking, moreover, of 'real' fashion as distinct and separate from 'written' (or 'described') fashion.

According to Julia Kristeva (1969), Barthes also intuitively sensed an aspect of fashion as ideologeme, as the function, that is, of linking the translinguistic practices in a society by compressing or concentrating the dominant mode of thought.

The concept of ideologeme, however, may now be assimilated in that of 'sign system' as the mediation between production modes and ideological institutions. While the ideologeme refers specifically to the text and the written word (even though, as Kristeva says, the text manipulates categories unknown to language), 'sign system' is a broader category that includes a non-verbal dimension.

I should like here to look at the fashion model as a sign system. The model, who maintains with the paper woman a relation of similarity and distinction: similarity in that she is *the model*, distinction in that Barthes' 'absolute body' becomes a sign exchanged in the worldly imagery of fashion. The taboo mentioned by Barthes – not signifying the body but the garment – is shattered: the mannequin's body no longer signifies merely the garment, but a whole world. The models are the new divas, distant stars, like the great Hollywood actresses of the Golden Age of cinema, who are yet known to everyone, and constructed in fashion discourse as a public space of universal discourse.

What's more, beyond the passage from paper model to 'spoken' or named model, there is another kind of passage, not temporal but semiotic: from the ideal automatic body (incarnated by the top model) to an everyday model of street fashion, in the dual sense, both metaphoric and literal, of street fashion. Metaphoric: the fashionable body as worldliness and popular culture, as unique yet universal language. Literal: the female body as constructed and in construction, product and process of representation and self-representation.

Let's begin with an image from the 1950s: Lisa Fonssangrives, immobile and sophisticated in evening gown and gloves. Triumphant, around her body the folds of a Balenciaga cloak, around her neck four strings of pearls. In a class of her own, even when she's lying on the lawn in jeans reading Gertrude Stein. The cigarette between her fingers has perhaps too much ash, but who knows when, for past, present and future cease to exist in the eternal instant of her pose. Lisa Fonssangrives incarnates the prototype of the Barthesian model *par excellence*. The garment as signified, existing without the body. The body as seat of the inorganic.

Walter Benjamin writes: 'Every fashion is in conflict with the organic. Every fashion couples the living body with the inorganic world. In fashion the rights of the corpse prevail over the rights of the living. Fetishism, underlying the sex appeal of the inorganic, is fashion's vital nerve' (Benjamin 1982: 124).

Clothing fetishisms spring from the power of merchandise to assume a mystical character, since it is the result of the transformation of a product of human activity into a thing, an object: 'Fashion is the means of transferring the character of merchandise to the cosmos ... fashion is the sex appeal of merchandise: the mobilisation of the inorganic through fashion, its triumph in the doll' (Benjamin 1982 : 70).

Benjamin also quotes Karl Gröber: 'To publicise better their fashion creations the resourceful Parisians used Models that attracted much attention: mannequin-dolls ... Once they had ended their time as Models, these dolls, which were still in use in the 17th and 18th centuries, were given to children as toys' (1982: 876). And Gutzkow in *Briefe aus Paris*: 'I had the strong suspicion that in some of the carriages, instead of the women who seemed to be sitting there, there were actually mannequins in shawls and silks and velvets ...' (1982: 877).

The social territory to which Benjamin refers is the same as that described by Proust's narrator, and the body of his imaginary corpse-model is, like Odette's body, made up of replaceable parts, an unstable architecture oscillating between 'nature' and 'technique': '... it was difficult to discern any continuity [in her body] given the fashion of the day, and Odette was one of the best dressed women in Paris ... the bust, projecting like a ledge over an imaginary stomach and ending brusquely in a point, while below the double petticoats billowed out like a balloon, gave the impression that the woman was composed of parts awkwardly fitted together' (Proust 1913: 240–1).

Odette is the top model of modernity, Barthes' perfect mannequin. The paradox of naming the body: an autopsy can be carried out on the automaton, a list drawn up of disassembled, unreal parts. But the body is not the Argos: its naming and substitution can only take place as mockery and parody. Barthes intuitively sensed this too, when he cited style as parody in fashion photography:

> ... the woman is caught in an amusing attitude, or better still, a comic one; her pose, her expression are excessive, caricatural; she spreads her legs exaggeratedly, miming astonishment to the point of childishness, plays with outmoded accessories (an old car), hoisting herself up onto a pedestal like a statue, six hats stacked on her head, etc. In short, she makes herself unreal by dint of mockery; this is the mad, the outrageous. (1967: 302)

And he adds in a note that the outrageous 'upsets the traditional fashion taboos: Art and Woman (Woman is not a comic object)'. So is she a tragic one?

In the two paintings by Frida Kahlo, *The Broken Column* (1944) and *The Tree of Hope* (1946), two items of an invalid's clothing are present: the leather corset supporting the spinal column and the white sheet draped over the woman's flanks and shoulders. The body is stripped, exposed, bare yet covered at the same time. There is a total continuity between the draped sheet and the inside of the body in *The Broken Column*, in which a marble column in place of the spinal column holds up the body-edifice. The nails are studs piercing both flesh and cloth, which are indistinguishable:

> ... of course, this is merely the result of the damned operation. Here I am seated at the edge of an abyss with the leather corset in my hand. And here I am again, lying on the hospital stretcher, while I look out at the landscape, part of my back uncovered, showing the scars that those bastard surgeons have made. (Letter to Eduaordo Murillo Safa, 11 October 1946)

Tears of a Mexican Madonna, experience marking the body: Frida Kahlo always rejected the epithet 'surrealist' for her work. Indeed, she creates a more-than-real model of herself, in which her experience even clothes her inside. Whatever happened to the sealed, integral, smooth and clean body of anatomy?

Adrienne Rich writes: 'When I write "my body" I see nothing in particular. To write "my body" plunges me into lived experience, particularity: I sees scars, disfigurements, discolorations, damages, losses, as well as what pleases me. White skin, marked and scarred by three pregnancies, a sterilisation, progressive arthritis, four joint operations, calcium deposits, no rapes, no abortions, much time at the typewriter, and so forth' (Rich 1985: 10).

What the institutional mannequin represents is something quite different from this form of self-representation, in which parody and realism in the depiction of time and the body enter into play. The fashion system, on the other hand, constructs stereotypes of female beauty through the symbolic economy of the model. For Ugo Volli, the multiplication and diffusion of what he calls the 'absent fascination of the Model' on social territory simply fuel the shallow, sterile and arid cult of a female image devoid of a specific body and identity (Volli 1992: 218–19). The stereotype is inescapable, for it is based on acritical repetition, ideologized allusion and received meaning. In the fashion system, however, the stereotype encounters difficulties in the very moment of its inception: on the one hand, fashion seems to assert its constructions of a female body based on that of the mannequin; on the other, the mannequin's body, as a body subjected to the garment-as-signified, transcends its own limits and so paradoxically transcends any stereotyped crystallization of meaning.

Classic examples of this are Twiggy, Jean Shrimpton and Penelope Tree. In other words, the moment models began to be called by name, they began to signify not only the garment, but also themselves, or better, what they were expected to signify, based on a reinvention of the body; for example, in Twiggy's case, as absurdly thin. Yet it was *that* body specifically and no longer a *generalized* one.[2] Even earlier, Coco Chanel 'seem[ed] to epitomize the liberated woman of the 1920s' (Steele 1993: 122). Her body was completely reinvented by fashion and reproduced as the symbol of the *new woman*.

Isabella Rossellini, who began modelling late, is something of a special case, since her body is fundamentally her face. Perhaps hers is the absurd destiny of being, literally, the daughter of Hollywood and Neorealism. Today, at over forty, she represents the irony of the automatic body and her makeup has to reckon with both her 'freshly scrubbed' type of beauty and her age. Even in the most 'composed' photographs for Lancôme her face constantly expresses the play of masks that animates it. Her years subvert the rigid criterion of youthfulness in the world of the top model, while her short hair plays at following the latest trend and at citation (perhaps her mother in *Joan of Arc* or *For Whom the Bell Tolls*). She is the transparency of the face, impossible to dissect; the face as contact, invitation ... and body. The further her face is from classical canons, the closer it comes to the everyday, while the more it exhibits citation and resemblance, the more it is absolutely unique. With her million-dollar contracts – or in spite of them? – Isabella Rossellini would seem to represent the passage from top to pop model.

Millions of dollars: hardly of minor importance in the phenomenology of the model, especially the institutional model of the 1990s. The form assumed by the exchange of women in the actual gender division of sign-work passes through the model's body. Pierre Klossowski has coined an effective expression to define the 'industrial slave' (showgirl, hostess, model): 'living money'. The body as something more than just merchandise, the body as money *tout court*: '... the industrial slave is a sign guaranteeing wealth and, at the same time, is herself wealth' (Klossowski 1970: 82). And he continues: '... the bodily presence is already merchandise, independently of and *more so* than the commodities that such merchandise helps to produce. The industrial slave either establishes a close relation between her bodily presence and the money it makes, or substitutes her body for money; her body thus *becomes* money, simultaneously both the equivalent of wealth and itself wealth' (84).

Thus a kind of vicious circle is set up between the job of this industrial slave[3] and her body as a special kind of merchandise, the equivalent of money. The experience of many 'mannequins' would seem to confirm this: for example, Benedetta Barzini, a famous model from the 1960s, today a writer and journalist, exposes the world and work of the model in her novel *Storia di una passione senza corpo*, defining it as being 'at the mercy of waiting for a phone call'.

This vicious circle would seem to be confirmed, moreover, by the role of top models in mass imagery and public communication, both for what is said about them and for what they say about themselves. They appear to have nothing of the old woman-object about them, since they are presented as the best managers both of themselves and of their colossal fortune, especially in view of harder times, with 'old age' bearing down on them at dizzy speed. Like actresses, they won't risk any identification with their *dramatis persona*, since they are themselves pure *personae*, conforming absolutely to their worldly performance. And herein lies the risk the top model runs of losing a 't' for a 'p', 'top' for 'pop'. A play on words, true, but only to a certain extent. The transformation of the mannequin's ideal body into the everyday body of the pop model has to do with the fact that the sign system of fashion has itself been transformed into a worldly system.

Putting on clothes means acknowledging the laws governing fashion imagery and circulating the body in the world. This form of resemblance generates an image of the body similar to Young Werther's (as described by Barthes in *Fragments of a Lover's Discourse*) for whom clothes indicate his nearness to the loved one:

> I desire to be the other and the other to be me, as if we were one, closed within the same skin, since the garment is merely the smooth outer shell of that coalescent material of which my amorous imagination is made. (Barthes 1977:15)

The garment as a vessel of otherness, a place where the identity of one's body is confused, an indistinct zone between covering and image. In this respect, the 'worldly' may be taken as the place where covering, style, image and *look* go beyond fashion, while still retaining some of its traits.

The clothed body, the body-as-covering, and its imagery burst into social territory. This hyper-semiotic connotation of the body is the condition for the latter's creating a narrative, communicative space, one produced by a symbolic body that is, paradoxically, unique and non-reproducible, even though it is reproduced as image.

Mario Perniola writes that the contemporary *look* creates a 'landscape', a timeless space for classical fashion and anti-fashion, both phenomena that claim to interpret and represent (Perniola 1990: 58–9). In its worldly guises, the body undergoes a passage from automatic to mutant body, and in this passage the meaning of 'fashion' is closer to the Latin root of the Italian 'moda' – *modus* or 'measure' – with its strong ethical implications. Collocated in a space of cohabitation and exchange with other bodies, the body takes on relational values that produce lifestyles and express – at the level of aesthetic choice – behavioural patterns and aspirations which otherwise would not be 'with the times' except in a conventional sense.

The mutant body is part of the cyborg metaphor. For Donna Haraway the cyborg is a creature from science fiction, a postmodern metaphor but also a reality of the late twentieth century in which 'we are all chimeras, theorised and fabricated hybrids of machine and organism' (Haraway 1991: 150). The cyborg is a hybrid that represents the dream of a 'powerful infidel hetereoglossia' (Haraway 1991: 181). Haraway sees the cyborg body as a product determined by the material social reality of our age – 'the cyborg is our ontology,' she writes – but also as a challenge to that very same reality, to the division of labour, dualism, gender and ethnocentricity. Despite the fact that for Haraway the cyborg is a purely postmodern phenomenon, we can nevertheless isolate two aspects of this image of the body which do not fall exclusively under the aegis of postmodernity: irony and the grotesque.

Irony allows the body, like discourse, to 'play on the edge' (to paraphrase Bakhtin), to avoid closure and containment, while the grotesque is ambivalence, metamorphosis and openness of the body. All elements which clothes make possible through the sign system of fashion. All elements which transform the ascetic top model into a grotesque, cyborg pop model.

A constant sliding between woman as representation and object of representation, on the one hand, and woman as historical being and relational subject, on the other. As Teresa de Laurentis writes: 'women are both inside and outside gender, at once within and without representation' (1987: 10).

Transvestism: in the refined 'performance' of Jaye Davidson in *The Crying Game* the dissonance between sex and gender is imperceptible. The so-called 'natural' representation of femininity is not camped up; what is exhibited is rather the de-naturalization of the presumed identification between (biological) sex and (cultural, semiotic) gender, as well as the dramatization of the cultural mechanisms presiding over their fictitious unity (see Butler 1990).

According to the African-American feminist writer, bell hooks, there is a close relation between style, as expressed by clothes, and subversion, that is, the way in which throughout American history both 'master' and 'servant' have used style to express respectively either conformity to or resistance against the dominant social order (hooks 1990: 217).

The concept of style has been interpreted by Susan Kaiser (1992) as something that both includes and transcends institutional fashion, since it has to do with the relation between experience and identity, and is 'a strategy used to express both a cultural aesthetic *and* an acquisition of power' (Kaiser 1992: 187), especially in African-American appearance styles.

The black top/pop model's body is constructed by the obsessive gaze of white westerners: for example, the 'perverse' fascination of a Grace Jones or the 'animal-like' beauty of a Naomi Campbell. An ambiguous process, since the values at stake in the construction of these clichés of female beauty are indeed prescriptive and objectifying, and yet the figure of the black model, idealized by white men and women alike, has allowed the construction of a cultural space for interaction between bodies that transcends physical and sexual race stereotypes.

The pop model is everywhere and everyone; she is a semiotic subject in process, in 'continuous clothing' we might say. While partaking of the social technologies of gender and metaphysical beauty (commonplaces of women and fashion), she is nevertheless distinct both from the representation of the 'essence' of femininity and from the woman as a subject determined by the social technologies of gender. She is a figure of passage between different bodies, as well as between different reference points and zones of imagination and knowledge.

Notes

1. I refer here to the distinction drawn by Charles Morris: see Morris 1964.

2. A famous model from the 1970s, Patti Hansen, went from the pages of *Vogue* to play the part of a taxi-driver in *They All Laughed* in which, at one point, someone says to her "You could be a model, you know".

3. "Slave" is an excessive term, says Klossowski, since the work is freely chosen.

6

The Face and the Gaze

The fascination of the gaze: a vague allure, a dim recognition in the shape of the face, a hint of a dialogue with the other's gaze. But a risk too: precipitating into the arms of Death with no return, like Eurydice saved and lost again by Orpheus, who looks back at her too soon; or the risk of being turned to stone by the Medusa's stare.

In every human experience the gaze leads to irreversible situations, signalling the passage to a state in which everything seems final. Looking is both changing the world and others, and being changed in turn by their gaze. A gaze which is never direct, however, but always mediated, deviated, if not impeded by the veil of our knowledge, dreams and projections onto the world, images at the intersection of which the 'I' that both looks and is looked at takes shape. The veil, the covering, is textile and garment, but first and foremost it is cultural textile-text, if we take 'culture' to mean all the material that goes to make up human thought, language and behaviour. Fashion intervenes to mark ideologically this cultural material, without which fashion itself could not exist.[1]

Then there's always the danger of meeting Actaeon's fate, changed into a stag by Diana when he came upon her bathing. 'Now go and tell them that you've seen me unveiled, if you can,' Diana challenges him, thus celebrating in myth the other risk brought by the gaze, that of becoming mute, a state close to death, given that Actaeon as a stag is torn to pieces by his own hounds. Yet another moral: the female body, represented by the virginal Diana, is veiled with knowledge and yet, when unveiled, gives no access to its own particular truth[2] and doesn't even allow men to speak about it. Thus woman weaves the final veil, the death shroud, for the male presumption of telling the truth about a body which is in continuous flux between naked and veiled, garment and skin.

More than any other textile, the veil simultaneously fulfils two functions: that of creating an interaction between clothes and body, a function common to almost every type of covering, and that of exhibiting nakedness through concealment. Yet another irony of clothing, taken up periodically by fashion in the use of voile, chiffon and organza, textiles in which there is a play of transparencies and prohibited gazing. If the veiled body, like the clothed body, is today a non-naked body, the fascination of which lies in playing hide and seek with beauty, as Nietzsche says, then there is a part of the body which presents itself as naked *par excellence*, even from under the mask of makeup: the face.

Perhaps we can speak of the face's nakedness because we learn to recognize others especially by their face. It's more difficult to recognize a person by other parts of their body or their gestures: for example, let your gaze fall on their hands or way of walking, concentrate on their voice or the stylistic flourish in a billet-doux from a virtual lover ... lovers' secrets, these, or the prerogative of astute observers. Gazing at the face is, above all, seeking the other's gaze. This 'face-to-face' goes beyond mirror-like reflection, though it may recall it, and goes beyond the identity of self. Gazing into another's eyes always brings with it a deflection from the flatness of the reflected image to the refraction of a dialogue.

The veil over the face is foreign to western culture, perhaps because the western 'subject' is constructed largely on reciprocal gazing. Nevertheless, every culture is formed by looking at what is distant, and by constantly looking to the past as a time to regain. Fashion is fully aware of this prerogative and today stands at the intersection between cultures world-wide, and between themes that bring together past and present, sacred and profane, near and far. The gaze may be deviated yet again and the face veiled to excess by the thick warm fabric of a *cagoule*. A Tuareg citation, perhaps?

In Islam the veil for women was introduced by the caliph Omar, who based his 'invention' on certain verses in the Koran which recommend that women lower their gaze and cover their head in public. The Tunisian scholar, Majid El-Houssi, has demonstrated that the use of the veil for women is closely linked to the importance of the gaze in the Islamic world (1987: 20). Being Muslim means controlling your gaze and maintaining a rigid divide between male and female. A woman's intimacy is protected by her veil; and in Islamic tradition this intimacy is called *'awra*, the root of which (*'awr*) means the 'loss of an eye', as El-Houssi points out, recalling the relation between prohibited sight and loss of sight. In the *Hadith* the punishment recommended for men who look at women not related to them is loss of the faculties of sight, touch and smell. In her analysis of the veil in Islam, Fadwa El Guindi (1999a) looks at the complex relations between the traditional religious dress code for women in different Muslim societies and the hierarchies of power, women negotiating their independence and aesthetics. In Islam the gaze is perversion of the eye, its interdiction, its *zina*, just as the word is the *zina* of language, physical contact the *zina* of hands and walking in desire the *zina* of feet. Only poetry, at once within and without laws and interdictions, can celebrate the gaze and voyeurism.

Indeed El-Houssi writes that Arabian secular poetry is a hymn to the eyes and a symphony to the gaze, where love can blossom from the mere glimpse of a portrait. The Muslim woman's veil thus originates in a cultural ambivalence: on the one hand, the gaze is prohibited, while on the other it is evoked by the fascination of what is hidden and by the tantalizing allusions in literature inspired by the jasmine-scented harem.

In Judeo-Christian tradition, on the other hand, the woman is veiled only for the marriage ceremony: 'thou hast doves' eyes within thy [veil] ... as a piece of pomegranate are thy temples within thy [veil]' (Song of Songs 4.1, 6.7). Greek and Roman brides were veiled too; indeed, the Latin word *nubere* meaning 'to veil' also meant 'to marry'. The veil of the Christian bride thus derives from this tradition, which links the Hebrew, Greek and Roman worlds. The veil as symbol of chastity and modesty, unveiling as symbol of an irreversible step: loss of virginity. Today the bridal veil survives in form, not in content.

If the nuptial veil is symbolically linked to sexuality, as an invitation to the bridegroom to dis-cover both face and sex, the Christian conventual veil derives instead from the *suffibulum* of Roman vestal virgins, which covers the head but leaves the face uncovered, with considerable loss of fascination, one might add. 'Taking the veil' means renouncing one's sexuality, subsuming it in one's love of God. To just what extent this may slide into eroticism is given eloquent testimony by Bernini's sculptural group of *The Ecstasy of St Theresa*.

In Medieval and Renaissance iconography, the Madonna is depicted with a veil over her head; it is often blue – though lined with black for the Mater Dolorosa, prototype of the Christian woman veiled in mourning – and enriched with gold and precious stones, as this Pauline prescription for women in prayer was gradually transformed from a sign of submission into one of refined elegance.

The veil over the face is thus a key concept in Christianity: the bridal veil, the mourning veil, and the other extreme, the Veronica Veil, with an impression of Christ's face on it. This veil is traditionally attributed with healing properties associated with the legend of Veronica relieving Christ's suffering on Golgotha, which is in its turn associated with the apostles' account of Christ healing a sick woman. Moreover, in Medieval legend, Christ's image on the veil was said to have healed the Emperor Tiberius when he placed it on his face. A thaumaturgic veil by proxy: blood and the image of the Saviour's face placed over a human face like a mask. Here the fascination lies in the eternal seduction of Death regenerating whoever touches it, not with their hands but with their face or eyes, which are perhaps the parts we least like having touched.

Yet we do indeed 'touch' with our eyes and if they are left uncovered by the Islamic veil, the western fashion *à la belle epoque* of a short veil worn over a hat both veils and unveils them. Veiled eyes are large, languid and unfathomable, mesmerizing behind the caress of an ostrich boa, the face half-hidden by sumptuous fabrics, as in a Klimt painting. So what happens to the gaze when the mechanical apparatus of a pair of glasses is placed in front of the eyes?

Of all the masks ever invented for the face, glasses are generally those most motivated by a practical need. Nevertheless, ever since they were introduced to the West between the twelfth and thirteenth centuries (Marco Polo recounts that in China they were already in use at the court of Kubla Khan) the practical function has had to come to terms with an aesthetic function, as we can clearly see in early modern portraits of nobles and notables. The aesthetic function introduces fashion details even in the lenses, details that dictate shape, colour and type of material.

There is traditionally an unbridgeable gulf between glasses and feminine charm: for example, a short-sighted Marilyn Monroe in *How to Marry a Millionaire* constantly hides hers in order better to seduce an ageing financier. And again, Hitchcock uses glasses on women in many of his films in order to highlight the contrast between sex appeal and lack of it, as in *Vertigo*, or in order to portray a female character as 'bad'. But even these unattractive connotations of female eyewear must inevitably intersect with their opposite: the undeniable fascination emanating from a pair of eyes hidden behind dark glasses.

Summer brings to the fore the omnipresent vision of faces obscured by dark glasses, even though their season is really eternal, especially in the sunny climates of the Mediterranean. Sunglasses were invented at the end of the nineteenth century, though the fashion for dark lenses only really took off in the 1930s. Their success coincided with a decline in the use of broad-brimmed hats and bonnets in women's fashion. Sunglasses with black frames and lenses à la Blues Brothers even precede the irreverent blues duo, who turned them into a parodic and stylized sign. Parodic in that they derided the role of this type of sunglasses in the jet set's wardrobe and stylized in that they transformed into a fashion and a cult object what idols like Ray Charles (who appears in the film) and Stevie Wonder used out of necessity.

In the golden world of Hollywood stars, dark heart-shaped lenses evoke the 1950s image of Kubrick's Lolita or voluptuous young maidens in search of success in the age of the baby-boom. In the history of youth styles, on the other hand, illustrious exponents of the fashion for thick-rimmed dark glasses were the British Mods, who adopted them as part of their exaggerated collegiate style at the end of the 1950s. In the same period, a pair of expensive and well-made dark glasses appeared on Marcello Mastroianni's nose in *La Dolce Vita*, while in a famous Martini advertisement that humorously cites characters like Mastroianni, Onassis and Anita Eckberg, recreating the atmosphere of those years between Via Veneto and Portofino, the characters wear dark glasses, dangerous vehicles of mystery, betrayal and complicity.

Though invented to satisfy the practical need of protecting our eyes from the sun's rays, dark glasses have become a particular kind of fashion item, hiding or veiling the area around the eyes, and thus modifying salient facial features, often to the point of making a person unrecognizable. Indeed, the expression 'I didn't recognize you with those glasses on' is a common one, and when we meet someone in the street good manners prescribe taking off our sunglasses so that we can look and be looked at directly. Unless, of course, we deliberately want to mask our gaze; for example, if we feel embarrassed or are crying, or simply want to hide our identity. There has even been a bizarre fashion recently for mirror lenses, not only in the mountains, where they make sense, but also in the city, the effect of which is simply to add a vulgar touch to the face.

Since the 1970s sunglasses have been synonymous with the name Ray Ban, the American company that not only introduced the famous pear-shaped model, but also inaugurated the fashion for sunglasses with a label, like Lacoste for shirts and Levi's for jeans.

Despite the introduction of different models to suit different tastes, in the last decade the Ray Ban constellation has been obfuscated by the avant-garde models of the new cult sunglasses, Web. Known above all for the celebrities who wear them, Web glasses effectively represent anti-Ray Bans, since they experiment with ostensibly 'poor' materials and bizarre shapes, producing a 'baroque' effect, whereas Ray Bans represent a more 'classical' style. Rough metal, screws sticking out, spirals connecting the lenses; everything exhibits a subtle wit and playful irony of design that guarantee an enthusiastic public of affluent, yet non-eccentric buyers.

Apart from these successful name brands, in the context of Italian production (which has recently broken all sales records) lenses for all tastes and ages fill the shop windows, and not just the optician's. Indeed, the latest fashion is for shops that just sell dark glasses. The most 'pop' models of the moment have big, mask-like lenses with titanium or transparent tube frames. And the habit of wearing sports glasses (in the shape of swimming goggles or cyclist's glasses) is on the increase too: there is even a prototype with a rear-view mirror for pedestrians at risk in city traffic! In the near future we will probably witness an advance in the technological function of sunglasses, which will not only shield our eyes from the sun, but also serve as a telecommunication instrument or a computer running on solar energy.

The face is masked, the face as mask. What lies behind that smooth brown skin, those elongated eyes and thick eyebrows, that round red mouth and bobbed hair? Perhaps nothing more than the act itself of hiding something. The idea of a bare face to be inscribed with the 'signs' of makeup ignores the fact that such nakedness is already inscribed, scored by a thousand tales alluding to age, nutrition, medicine, love, origins and so on.

Retracing history and searching in the genealogy of the face for something that might help us understand its phenomenology, a concept stands out: *facies*, the surface appearance characterizing a type, which ancient medicine read as signs referring to the body's general state and its collocation in space. The face as moveable territory, whose signs Hippocratic medicine, exemplified by the work of Galen, scrutinized, not in terms of anatomy, but of their connection with the surrounding world and with one another, in that state of otherness and oneness intrinsic to every living being. Yet those signs were regulated by a strict morality: in Galen physical health (of face and body), the source of all 'natural' beauty, is opposed to 'false' beauty obtained through strange artifice. *Cosmetica-commotica*: Plato clearly distinguishes between the two, linking the art of cosmetics to rhetoric, sophistry and the culinary arts, while care of the body is linked to gymnastics, medicine and dialectics. The Platonic condemnation of makeup poses the problem of legitimacy as one of truth – or vice versa.

Nevertheless, ancient medicine wasn't able to draw a precise boundary between the two arts: bodily health requires remedies that waver between nature and artifice, and thus Galen's prescriptions for lightening the face or smoothing the skin are implicitly inspired by a philosophy of beauty as construct and culture, not nature. For classical writers, makeup was part of the art of seduction, whether for courtesans or in literary transpositions of the *ars amatoria*. Ovid ignores morality and nature and praises makeup as part of sensual, narcissistic pleasures – *est etiam placuisse sibi quaecumque voluptas* – and he collects recipes and prescriptions for beauty treatments that have all the 'flavour' of culinary recipes. Irony at Plato's expense: *commotica* and gastronomy?

A healthy face thus seems inevitably linked to writing, whether directly on its surface, or in the prescribing and describing of makeup. The prescription evades the norm, however, and is always accompanied by a 'degustation', as in culinary recipes, that relies on memory and the description of the way in which the recipe was followed on a particular occasion (an occasion that may turn out to be unique and unrepeatable, but nevertheless may be transcribed).

Makeup is the beauty of the face taken to excess, in the total arbitrariness of the signs exhibited on it. The use of cosmetics is an art that does not have the same transforming power and significance as theatrical makeup, and it is perhaps this delicacy and precariousness that make it 'feminine'. In *L'éloge du maquillage* Baudelaire commends the female privilege of borrowing from all the arts the means to rise above nature through the sovereign art of makeup. For Baudelaire (1863: 306) nature is but an evil advisor that leads men to commit heinous crimes, whereas virtue lies in artifice, and hence in makeup, clothes and elaborate hairstyles. Furthermore, writes Baudelaire, those societies considered 'close to nature' by the European mind reveal an understanding of the profound spirituality of artifice and disguise, as shown by their attraction for all that glistens, for colourful plumage, artificial forms, face painting, masks and so on. The western idea of nature is thus far from the 'primitive' and 'natural' societies of which Baudelaire speaks; it is a mythical horizon which is itself the product of artifice and invention.

Makeup plays with nature in those parts of the face that are most exposed to the world: skin, eyes and mouth. The skin: a discreet involucrum in its folds, wrinkles, colouring and texture. The eyes: the gaze bestows them immediately on the other, even before that 'other' has been seen or recognized. The mouth accompanies three important moments in the relations between bodies: speaking, eating and love-making. In emphasizing writing and colour, in replenishing the skin and covering the face, makeup paradoxically recalls the face's authentic nakedness. The link between makeup and seduction cannot be banally summed up in terms of enticement and provocation; the nakedness evoked by makeup is the erotic nakedness of the female face, called by the philosopher of otherness, Emmanuel Lévinas, perturbation, invasion of non-significance in the significance of the face (Lévinas 1974). The face is a sign of recognition, a surface patina exposed to relations, its identity is contaminated by apertures that expose it to the world: a symptom, a blush, a grimace. Makeup treats these apertures ironically and invests female beauty with a mixture of chastity and obscenity, containment and immoderation.

Barthes discerned in Japanese theatre, especially in kabuki, the emptiness of the made-up face (1970: 107). The actors in kabuki, all men, paint their faces with a heavy white substance, which reduces the face to an 'empty expanse of white stuff' (Barthes 1970: 105) onto which the elongated slits of eyes and mouth are incised. The absence of meaning in this face is due to a total absence of expressiveness, to a writing that says 'nothing'

(Barthes 1970: 107). In the West, on the other hand, it is the superabundance of signs inscribed on the face that renders them 'intransitive', devoid of any possible equivalence.

In makeup we can identify two ways of 'writing' the face: the imperceptible, that concentrates on the skin to make it smoother and more luminous, and the graphic, or conspicuous, that accentuates contours and colours. The dividing line between imperceptible and graphic is by no means clear, however: a mascara may lengthen and thicken the lashes, miming an invisible naturalness, while a foundation may be particularly dense and so openly declare its presence on the face. Even curative cosmetics may have a graphic effect: for example, by restoring compactness to mature skin. And if exaggerated, with the use of sunlamps, even the 'natural' and curative effect of a suntan may become graphic.

Fashion, that legislator without laws, that sign of the times outside time, regulates the forms of cosmetic art. The ethics of fashion, which for Baudelaire resided in a taste for the ideal, has transformed that ideal into one of a replaceability of signs, not as an equal exchange, but as a 'waiting for the next one', according to Heidegger, given the rhythms of anticipation and fascination with the moment that go to create an 'instantaneous' body, whose fragmentary replaceability supplants both wear-and-tear and ageing. Heidegger writes:

> Today being means being replaceable ... in the phenomenon of fashion, toilette and ornament are no longer necessary (which is why fashion as toilette has become as obsolete as mending) but the replaceability of the model from season to season. We no longer change a garment because it is worn-out, but because it has the specific character of being the garment of the moment, waiting for the next one. (Heidegger, 1977: 107)

In this economy of the body, in the eternal waiting for a replacement, mending and repairing only find a place if they challenge time. Today makeup takes this law to its extreme: not only is makeup an eternally replaceable mask in its graphic dimension, but it creates a constant structural mutability in the face, even if simply curative. A cream for wrinkles or spots, a hair dye, a vial to combat dry skin: today the challenge is to get there first, to stop time, in a state of ecstatic expectation. Will the skin dry out again if we stop using that lotion, is the natural colour of the hair peeping out at the roots? Is the artificial body perhaps menaced by nature? Or can we write the face not just with artifice, but with fatigue, wrinkles and neglect? This too is part of the game, since buffoonery, irony and self-irony all have a place in the world of fashion today.

Nature and artifice contaminate each other and cosmetics today cite living organisms: algae, placenta, herbs, milk and so on. This new game recalls ancient remedies conserved in folklore, witchcraft and ballads, where some of the ingredients were even 'baser' (blood, excrement), but also comprised herbs, flowers and honey. As if the organic analogy, whether in the ancient alchemist's laboratory or the modern chemical company, could serve to cure or disguise the face through an inversion of the life flow, regenerating life through death.

Notes

1. Fashion and clothes have always been related to 'futile' problems that nevertheless point to more serious philosophical and cultural issues. The notion of truth, for example, a fundamental problem in western philosophy, was called by the Greeks *aletheia*, at once revelation and concealment; and this bodily and conceptual play of revealed and concealed is at the heart of much western philosophy and literature.

2. In traditional allegorical representation Truth is a naked woman.

7

Degree Zero of Fashion and the Body: The Model, the Nude and the Doll

At the beginning of the new millennium fashion speaks a global language: the sometimes real, but more often imaginary utilization and enjoyment of its signs transcends continental, social and ethnic barriers, since these signs follow the laws of the object and image market, which we consider universal. The specific qualities of fashion items (colour, design, material, etc.) are of secondary importance compared to the simple fact of their being *on the market* and, more especially, compared to the fact that, in this exchange of images, it is the body that is in circulation. Specifically models' bodies – the new divas, the new stars. Until the 1960s (when the oldest of today's top models were probably not even born) the 'mannequins' were, as Roland Barthes (1967: 259) writes, the 'pure forms' whose role was to signify not the body but the garment (see Calefato 1996: 88–100). Their role, though star-like for some (for instance, Twiggy, Jean Shrimpton and Patti Hansen), was linked to a clearly defined sector of the market and of communication, which was the world of fashion up to that time. Barthes attributed to the cover-girls, or mannequins, the role of representing a synthesis of dress and costume, that is, both an individual phenomenon and a socially regulated value system. Barthes writes that in a garment from a designer collection there are traces of dress linked, for example, to the size and shape of the model wearing it, but these are of slight importance since 'the ultimate aim of the garment is, in this case, that of representing a costume' (Barthes 1998: 68).

Today the taboo highlighted by Barthes – not signifying the body but the garment – has been violated and the models, products and emblems of fashion as a triumphant and luxurious sector of mass communication, have undoubtedly taken the place once occupied in social imagery by actresses. Like the great Hollywood divas, these mannequins are, for the public, distant, unreachable stars, and yet they are known to us down to the smallest detail, manipulated, and gossiped about like old friends. Their names are on everyone's lips, often accompanied by adjectives and definitions which label their image. Newspapers, magazine covers, calendars, television commercials and programmes exhibit them in every conceivable form.

More than fashion models, they are models to emulate for the many women who see in them a female ideal that brings together beauty, self-transformational skills, wealth and business sense. In the 1960s an army of perfectly formed girls dreamed of becoming Miss World or of flying to Hollywood to be the next Marilyn Monroe, whereas today teenagers, be they well-fed by our opulent society or less fortunate youngsters from the Third World, dream of becoming top models. How many of them succeed in this race and how many fall by the wayside? Above all, what kind of female model is this, how and why does it reach the younger generations? Much is due to the indisputable beauty of these women, which did not used to be so important (take Twiggy, who certainly was not beautiful in the canonic sense), and which comes across in the communication of images. The seductive power of the image is an important stimulus in the construction of contemporary myth. The construction of the image is, at the same time, the construction of the body: a fact which makes the myth of the top model somewhat different from that of the film star, who ran the risk of being forever identified with the character that made her famous. The mannequin's body follows the postmodern destiny of being transformed into a thing, an object through which values, meanings and desires are circulated.

Yet perhaps the girls we meet on the street, who fill the schools and universities, the everyday pop models (Calefato 1996: 100), the women of all ages who play the game of appearance styles, manage to adapt fashion to their bodies in its freest component, as a vehicle of experiences and sensations. Rather than thinking of bodies that have become things, perhaps it would be more interesting to think of things that have become bodies, to think of objects as living bodies of high cultural, ethical and aesthetic definition. And so, to try to bring to life the fashion objects and signs that surround us, in the daily construction of a *look*, as bodies with which we enter into contact.

If Andy Warhol were still alive today he would no doubt have enjoyed exhibiting in a multiple image a photograph of Courbet's highly acclaimed painting *L'origine du monde*, a painting much commented on by the media and academics, which shows in extreme close-up and with incredible realism a female pubis. The American artist would have had fun mocking, but at the same time consecrating, the perverse mechanism in our society of images, thanks to which it has become more and more difficult to make a valid or clear distinction between works of art and consumer images. In this case, for example, to distinguish between Courbet's masterpiece and Sharon Stone's private parts in *Basic Instinct*, since both form an undifferentiated part of mass media communication and aesthetic enjoyment. Warhol multiplied Marilyn Monroe's face, and later, shortly before his death, he dedicated his serial portraits to great Italian designers, foreseeing that the excesses within the fashion system would soon have a lot to say about human behaviour, taste and received meaning.

Summer is the season for celebrating the human body in its varying degrees of nudity. The time when magazines enjoy overwhelming us with pounds of flesh snapped by the merciless *paparazzi*, when the streets and beaches are filled with thighs, buttocks, stomachs, smooth chests, hairy chests, and breasts that have left the Wonderbra at home. And every season the mass media hold up female nudity as a metaphor for everything from political elections to advertisements for glue. Recently, however, there has undoubtedly been a quality jump in the public portrayal of the naked body, which can only be due to the fact that there are more and more images of male nudes around to be enjoyed.

Yet, how is it that after decades of women being objects of representation, and of general disapproval for the few who dared to show themselves naked, female flesh has nothing more to offer to the masses, while there is still a lot to discover under men's clothing? How has this almost total reversal of taste crept in, so that even fashion magazines and catwalks, both traditionally female domains, are opening their doors to the male nude?

Actually there were precursors, as is often the case, in cinema. Several years ago the smooth nudity of a young Chinese man engaged in long erotic feats with an adolescent Marguerite Duras in the film *L'amant* had a great effect. Many female cinema-goers were also struck by the rough terrain of Harvey Keitel's body being explored by Ada in *The Piano* directed by Jane Champion. Another female director, Antonia Bird, in the film *The Priest*, used the movie camera to construct a scene of total nudity in a male homosexual relationship, that even a heterosexual public, unaccustomed to explicit scenes of this type, found pleasantly erotic.

It was the English film *The Full Monty*, however, through the story of a group of unemployed men who set themselves up as strippers, that portrayed intelligently and ironically a strategy of social resistance and a redefinition of sexual roles. The main characters express an almost 'post-feminist' awareness in their disenchanted, grotesque use of the male striptease, with their 'everyday' bodies of every shape and size, a long way from the perfect muscles of professional strippers. One scene in particular reveals this awareness: while the main characters are tanning themselves on a sun bed and flicking through a magazine full of female nudes, one of them starts making comments about the women's bodies and another replies by asking how they would feel if women were to make similar comments about *their* naked bodies.

With his hardcore photos and 'obscene' close-ups, Robert Mapplethorpe was really the first artist of our times able literally to invent the male nude through a camera lens. Until recently, however, his message, censured as 'homosexual', had a relatively limited audience. Today advertisements for aftershave, showing the naked torsos of young men whom he would probably never have used as models, owe a lot to his art. 'Contrast' seems to be a key word in the success of the male nude. Especially an ideal contrast: the shock for the public (male and female alike) that has suddenly switched from perceiving the female nude as the height of eroticism, to the newly revealed frontiers of the nude male star.

The visual arts have always paid equal attention to the naked bodies of men and women: classical art and sculpture, at least until the seventeenth century, were full of male and female nudes in equal measure. Goddesses, nymphs and Madonnas with bared breasts accompany naked Christs, satyrs, male divinities and saints. Among these, the various versions of St. Sebastian, most famously those by Andrea Mantegna, undoubtedly catch the eye as prototypes of a certain kind of male nude which, even today, has a somewhat sadomasochistic connotation. It was in modern times, from the period Michel Foucault has called 'the classical age' – the end of the sixteenth, and the seventeenth and eighteenth centuries – that the portrayal of bodies began to distinguish between the sexes, following the western social hierarchy. Finally, in our age of mass communication, the female body has become the supreme sign and fetish object of public communication.

Actually the current success of the male nude has arrived late, given that no society in the West can still describe itself as being run by a group of white male heterosexuals. Women have consolidated their position and power, and gays are no longer 'in the closet'. Even 'straight' men have found inner qualities that their grandfathers would have branded 'feminine': tenderness in their relations with children, a certain dandyism, the appreciation of a beautiful body, irrespective of gender. All this produces a new kind of received meaning and multiplies the gaze through which images are constructed and tastes transformed. A man can finally refuse to give a lift to a Pamela Anderson lookalike standing by the roadside, as in the television commercial by a French car company. Likewise, women can slip banknotes into male strippers' G-strings, thereby emulating one of the less edifying male habits.

These images both record changes taking place in customs and add to them, as new frontiers of corporeality continue to open up: technological bodies, virtual bodies, inorganic bodies, silicon bodies, anabolic bodies and bodies transformed by plastic surgery. The naked body doesn't really exist, it is a *construction of representation*, be it photographic, filmic or off the drawing board; it is the result of beauty treatments, exercise, medical history and age; it is both product of and fuel for imagery. And today such imagery manifests itself in all its plurality and hybridization.

Many will remember the famous and heavily censured Benetton-Toscani advertisement with the newborn baby, naked, literally 'as her mother made her', even though her body was clothed in the natural 'shirt' we are all born with, the fluids that surround us in the womb. What better advertisement for a company selling all kinds of clothing, including shirts? No makeshift, artificial vest put on a newborn baby, bathed and doused in talcum powder, can compete with that slightly bloody, slightly transparent and slimy garment that, right from our entrance into the world, defines the 'lower limits' of the concept of human nakedness. When the advertisement came out, it provoked both instant acclaim and instant condemnation, because of the issue of whether or not it was acceptable to show the origins of life outside the mother's body so explicitly. What would children think? Perhaps it isn't true that the naked newborn body is simply that chubby, smooth, pink body we see in advertisements for nappies, creams and mineral water; it can also be the repelling image of a newborn alien letting out its first cry in the world. Just as its ugliness makes it all the more loveable in private, so it makes it all the more repugnant in public communication.

In a world overpopulated by images of young, healthy, sleek, tanned, muscular male and female nudes, energized by pills and body building, even modelled by silicone, there is no room for anyone who falls outside the limits of age, size or shape. Even though Marlon Brando, naked down to his groin with his overflowing paunch, can be tolerated, given that his popularity is based on gifts other than his body, neither the nakedness of the Benetton-Toscani baby nor, at the other extreme, that of the old or the sick can be used as conventional symbols to promote the prevailing idea of *the body* in our culture of mass communication.

Unless, of course, we are dealing with the absolute limits of nakedness that make it obscene, though not in a moralistic sense: the naked bodies of prisoners in concentration camps (in Nazi-occupied Europe and, more recently, in Bosnia), the war-wounded, the sick and the starving in the Third World, corpses, and so on. These kinds of images are usually used as historical documents, accusations, symbols and warnings, but they remain outside normal public consumption. Indeed, if we were to conjure up a mental image that represents the phrase 'the naked body', without even thinking about it, most would automatically visualize their favourite pin-up. Who would visualize the naked body of their eighty-year-old grand-mother, a terminally ill patient or an Argentinean *desaparecido*?

One television commercial, however, even dared to show an old lady naked in the bath, overdoing, perhaps, the grotesque effect of the lively granny in her colourful shower cap, her modesty preserved, nevertheless, by an abundance of bubbles. Better to cover up that presumably withered and wrinkled body. On the other hand, everyone loves the bare bottoms of TV toddlers and so we are obviously horrified when we read in the news-papers about acts of brutality committed against children; it seems unimag-inable that those little bodies in nappies could be violated.

The mass media representation of the body should be reassuring, honest and healthy; it should give the impression that the body is known inside-out by its owner, that its functions can be controlled and its anomalies modified. Some time ago there was a three-dimensional image on the Internet of a human body which had been completely penetrated by all the current scientific technology. It was more than naked, more than dissected, and was also an amazing computer spectacle, a virtual body, yet very real. Compared to this, the pictures of the autopsy of a supposed extraterrestrial recorded in utmost secrecy in America at the end of the 1940s and released to the public some time ago (who knows why) raise a smile. But perhaps they also make us think a little: the dissected alien, be it real or not, naked on the autopsy table, gives the impression of an old, helpless foetus. Newborn babies, aliens, the old and the sick are all alike: they make us think of a nakedness that is part of us all and that makes us, despite media reassurances to the contrary, a bit alien in our daily lives.

Watching her on television commercials can really get on your nerves; not her, Barbie, so much as those simpering little girls who smother her with endearments and caresses. As a doll she is not that bad, once you overcome your prejudices about the stereotype of female beauty that her perfect body represents. Even the most critical adults have come to believe that the most beloved doll of the second half of the twentieth century is not as harmful as they once thought. Partly because the ex-children who were the first to play with her have become mothers themselves, and partly because the messengers of doom concerning children's toys have forgotten her for the moment as they have recently started to rail against videogames and Internet. So Barbie is still the queen of little girls' daydreams. Little boys', too, given that 'new mums' and, more importantly, 'new dads' are learning not to repress the 'feminine' desires that their little boys might have for the sparkling dresses, mermaids' tails and flowing hair of this queen of dolls.

Cloned from Doris Day and Grace Kelly, and herself generatrix of Brooke Shields, there are people who have repeatedly undergone plastic surgery to look like her. Queen of worldly encounters, expert interior designer, refined model, boisterous sportswoman: Barbie is all this and more. That little face devoid of character, that unrealistic body, that image on TV in the most boring, most simpering advertisements unashamedly targeted at little girls, are undoubtedly questionable. It is pointless, however, to speak badly about her, because Barbie has become an object that can be loaded with every possible meaning, and not only in the play world of little girls.

An interesting aspect of this ideal female body is that, over the years, her face and size have been imperceptibly altered to reflect current trends in how the collective imagination has shaped the female body. In her early years she was more of a 'lady', becoming progressively more explosive and symbolic of a diet of homogenized products and oestrogen, while these days she has reverted to being more demure and almost new age.

It is not even true any longer that Barbie is white and blonde, perfectly WASP, because the Native American Barbie, a politically correct squaw, has been in production for some time. There are also, though with different names, African-American Barbie, Jamaican Barbie, Hispanic Barbie and United Colours of Benetton Barbie. Extra Large Barbie has also been launched; she has the same face, but is a little bit chubbier to reflect the increase of obesity amongst North American women. There is also a handicapped Barbie in a wheelchair. Thus in recent years a substantial force has been mobilized around Barbie to move her towards a soft form of political correctness and a sense of social responsibility.

A cult object and a collector's item for adults, too: there have been books and exhibitions dedicated to her, the doll museum in Paris was founded because of her, top designers such as Calvin Klein and Helmut Lang have created outfits for her. It is no longer true that she represents the archetypal 'dumb' blonde because, apart from her multi-ethnic transformations, Barbie has also started to talk. To be honest she only says a few silly phrases in a voice that is disappointing for those of us who had imagined her speaking like Marilyn Monroe, but she speaks nevertheless.

If Walter Benjamin could have lived another hundred years he would undoubtedly have written something about Barbie, since he considered dolls to be the hateful triumph of the inorganic (Benjamin 1982: 70). It is true, however, that the great German thinker was referring to the cut-out dolls used up to the nineteenth century to spread the latest Paris fashions, before specialist magazines were available *en masse*. Barbie too is 'useful' for contemporary fashion in a way. Little girls play with her as they used to play with paper dolls, whose silhouettes, clothed in a petticoat, could be dressed in endless combinations of clothes and hats. Famous designers put themselves to the test with 'Barbie's Boutique'; lesser known designers, too, like a certain Michael Alexander from Ohio, who invents extravagant outfits for this toy heroine. Some of the more exclusive Barbies, such as the one that looks like Elizabeth Taylor, are not available to the general public, but change hands amongst collectors for thousands of dollars.

So, is the prevailing image that of Barbie as the object of erotic-economic transactions and a merciless queen in the world of commerce? Or the image of a Barbie with a heart? This heart is certainly assigned to her in the everyday ritualistic games that children of both sexes, in every culture and society, have always played with dolls, whether it be the alabaster doll of the Babylonians, the wooden doll of the Egyptians, the Latin *pupa*, the *kachina* dolls of the American Indians, the Russian *matrioska* or the *bisquit* doll of modern Europe.

Unfortunately, a small blot has appeared on the doll's otherwise spotless curriculum vitae: for a short period in her life she succumbed to the pressure of a group of North American furriers and was seen wearing fur coats, stoles and accessories. This provoked the indignation of one association, PETA (People for the Ethical Treatment of Animals), which has successfully dedicated itself to making fashion representatives 'repent' for having worn or designed garments made with animal fur. A few years ago Naomi Campbell, Kate Moss and other famous top models stripped publicly on billboards and in magazines, declaring that they would rather go naked than wear fur. Now Barbie is ashamed of what the furriers made her do and is dedicating herself to an ecological turn around. 'Barbie doesn't wear fur because she loves animals' comes the timely announcement from the toy company that produces her. A declaration that has been welcomed by a whole generation of children educated from the cradle to despise the use of fur in fashion.

A few years ago one ecological campaign used an efficacious message aimed directly at children: a fluffy puppy saying 'Your mother has got a fur coat, mine hasn't any more'. The ecological emotive-persuasive effect was guaranteed. Today children and teenagers are undoubtedly the age groups most sensitive to an education that is not solely concerned with protecting animals, but ecological in every way. Flicking through magazines aimed at children we see that a lot of the articles and cartoons contain explicit messages about the protection of animals, messages that appeal to the sense of protection that every child, even the most helpless, needs to feel and cultivate towards a real puppy, a soft toy, or a whole species on the brink of extinction.

In 1946 Walt Disney could make *Peter and the Wolf* with scenes of the slaughtered wolf being brought back to the village by the hunters, whereas today this would no longer be possible, not unless, as in the case of *The Lion King*, the killing of the animal took place in a world where animals were the only protagonists, humanized in their emotions and passions. Remember that one of the most successful cartoon 'baddies' from the past is Cruella D'Evil, the bewitching fur fanatic from *101 Dalmatians* dressed in flamboyant furs, wicked pursuer of ninety-nine puppies whom she wants to turn into a fur coat.

So, a healthy aversion to those who exploit nature, not out of necessity but out of force of habit and luxury, has existed for some time in the consciousness of children. Today if Barbie, fetish object through whom all the symbols of fashion in the last decades have passed, sets herself up as a champion of the animal protection crusade, furriers and designers in that sector had better beware!

Barbie is of great importance to the youngest age groups as far as constructing an exterior identity based on clothing and care for one's body is concerned. Unlike her clones, who have invaded publicity, this is about the game of dressing her up, undressing her and dressing her up again, doing her hair, doing her makeup, adorning her with jewellery, and making the flexible version do difficult gymnastic movements. All these ritualistic games concern the establishment of taste and aesthetic sense. It then depends on many other factors whether the taste and aesthetic sense of the little girl or boy who play with Barbie manage to avoid stereotypes and pre-packed models later in life. The real responsibility of these models lies, not with Barbie and her make-believe world but with the real world, the world where multinational toy companies, while Barbie is carrying out her anti-fur campaign, continue to exploit human resources in their factories in the Far East.

An anthropologist in the year 3000 will probably study Barbie as one of the most common finds of the silicon age, along with jeans and mysterious, deteriorated celluloid tapes. In the meantime, without demonizing her or making her out to be a heroine, we can continue to reflect on how this object – at once a frozen and consumed image of the female body, fetish object, toy and symbol – can continue to be a prime player in the image game.

8

Intertextual Strategies and Contemporary Mythology

The imagery of the clothed body is produced through intertextual strategies in which fashion interacts with photography, journalism, music, sport, television, metropolitan culture, computers, design and cinema. The construction of the social signification of dress passes through widespread inter-semiotic practices which allow the construction and deconstruction of styles and tastes, a kind of navigating through signs where one can choose between a sense of belonging and travesty. In this form of communication fashion constructs its own worldly space (see Calefato 1992a, 1996) and produces a multidimensional world.

Garments become vehicles of desire, they take on social significations that draw on different communicative universes. Our desire to dress in a certain way (as a bridge to a certain life-style) is based on an emotional mechanism defined by Greimas (1983) as expectation, which puts the subject in relation to an object of value, in this case the garment, an object invested with value, or values, on the basis of social approval. Thanks to this social approval the value-laden object allows the subject to enter into relation with other subjects and the expectation to go from being 'simple' to being 'fiduciary' in that it presupposes just such a relation (Greimas 1983).

We can use the notion of expectation to interpret semiotically the expression 'removed meaning' used by Grant McCracken (1988) to indicate the sociocultural strategy through which consumer objects fill the gap between real and ideal in social life. In this mechanism emotional investment concerns multidimensional forms of sensation rooted in various social discourses. In this way objects in the consumer universe of fashion, objects comprising the generic whole Barthes calls 'dress' (1998: 66), become myths, in the sense of 'linguistic theft', of making natural something that has been culturally and socially constructed (Barthes 1957). Not only the *star system* and the system of glossy worldliness surrounding fashion today as a social institution, but the whole system itself of fashion objects belongs to this 'mythical' dimension present in the various social discourses through which fashion is expressed and circulated.

In his essays on contemporary mythologies, fifteen years after the publication of *Mythologies*, Barthes (1984: 67–8) clearly grasps the multi-dimensional and pluri-discursive nature of contemporary myth. Barthes tended to avoid the new catechism of post-1968 demystification, and this choice led him to construct new figures of discourse, new spaces for reflection on myth and communication. The figure of the 'idiolect', in particular, constituted a kind of ambivalent zone both for the reproduction of myth and resistance to it. The trans-textual system of signs and discourses that defines fashion today expresses itself through 'idiolects', that is, spaces within which the social subject anchors its identity to images and objects that circulate the body in society, while giving an impression of the uniqueness, exclusiveness and originality of every sign exhibited, every garment worn. Thus a close connection is established between the way in which the subject imagines and communicates his/her styles (life style, dress sense, way of thinking) and the perception of his/her social identity in all its multiple and negotiable forms.

So it becomes interesting to look at those aspects of the system which best represent unusual values and unexpected excesses. Not so much in terms of an ideological 'symbolic resistance' to myth and consumption, but rather in the search for an unstable tension between the logic of social reproduction and its aesthetic and sensorial reception and elaboration by social subjects.

Clothing is sometimes a way of dreaming an imaginary inhabitable world. From a linguistic point of view, this is expressed in the way in which the garment is metonymic with regard to the body: 'red shirt', for example, indicates both the garment and a member of Garibaldi's fleet and represents an exemplary mixture of clothing and utopia. An historical utopia, however much the two terms (history and utopia) may be at odds: the 'red shirt' belongs to a reality that actually happened, like its sister the 'white shirt' of Robespierre and Lenin, but also of Zapata and Goya's riflemen. Utopias of varying import, certainly, yet all utopias enough to make the 'white shirt' a positively evocative sign (unlike its opposite the 'black shirt'). The influence of this item on the imagery of dress is evident in contemporary men's fashion, where it is used by designers like Dolce & Gabbana, who are inspired by the traditional costume of Southern Italian men, those who were 'liberated' by the 'red shirts'.

There has always been a close relation between clothing and utopia for the simple reason that every utopia – whether in literature, philosophy or cinema – is populated by clothed human beings. A single 'emblem', an object such as a scarf, a brooch or a slogan on a T-shirt, can sometimes convey the passage to a utopian world. The meaning thus conveyed by these objects is no longer simply functional or practical, but a means of entry to the utopia of a body which is not ours, or of a world with which we share values and ideals and to which we feel we belong, perhaps depending on our adherence to a group.

The recommendation of a way of dressing as far away as possible from luxury and ostentation was characteristic of utopias in the past, like More's (1516) and Campanella's (1602); clothing was supposed to be comfortable and differed only according to the age and sex of the person wearing it. In Campanella's *La città del sole*, for example, the inhabitants wear a kind of toga over a white undergarment, knee length for the men and full length for the women. On the island of Utopia wool and linen fabrics are the most widely used, because of their purity. Silk is abhorred because it is too close to the dress aesthetic of More's own day, from which he was trying to distance himself. Francis Bacon's *New Atlantis* (1624), on the other hand, is inhabited by characters who seem to have stepped out of an oriental fancy dress party, in turbans and colourful baggy trousers (see A. Ribeiro, 1993).

In the nineteenth century women's trousers were considered a revolutionary garment by women who were just beginning to fight for their own utopia, their civil rights. Around the mid-nineteenth century across the Atlantic on the streets of New England, the famous bloomers appeared, the wide, calf-length trousers worn under a skirt and named after Amelia Bloomer, a women's rights activist, who was one of the first to wear them. Bloomers were also worn by members of the fifty or more utopian socialist communities inspired by the theories of Saint-Simon, Fourier and Owen, which emerged in America between 1820 and 1860.

In the twentieth century utopian foresight was entrusted to science fiction, beginning with the modern utopia created by H. G. Wells (1905), a critical disciple of Fabian socialism, who conceived his 'samurai', rulers (of both sexes) in an imaginary society, dressed in the style of the ancient Templars. Yet often the science fiction world is also the world of dystopias, like the well-known example from cinema, *Metropolis*, by Fritz Lang, where the inhabitants of the underground city, all depicted with their heads bowed because of the work to which they are submitted, are dressed in identical dark uniforms. A similar scenario is that of Orwell's *1984*, in which a blue boiler suit is prescribed for all party members. In Orwell's dark imaginary world the maximum simplification and homologation of clothing finds a parallel in the mono-thematic reduction wrought by the principles of the 'new language', which the English writer predicts will have substituted common language by around 2050.

For some historians of costume there is nothing further from fashion than utopia, since the goal of change in every utopia (or dystopia) is change *towards* an objective, whereas fashion follows an intrinsic law of change as *an end in itself* (Ribeiro 1993). Nevertheless, fashion, especially fashion that accompanies a 'narrative' – whether it be the caption in a specialized magazine or the reference to an historical style – always constructs a 'world theatre', a time and place which do not exist in reality, yet which are made to exist through the signs decreed by fashion. As examples of this 'world theatre' Barthes indicates fashion headlines like 'Muslin or taffeta for summer evenings' or 'Prints win at the races' (Barthes 1967: 34); and he defines a garment presented verbally or graphically in a fashion magazine as a true utopia (1998: 87 – note). To these fashion utopias and narratives we must add all those scenarios represented by styles, especially in youth culture, inspired by 'tribal' projects, or laws, which are antithetical to the institutionalized laws of dress and which, instead, tune into fantastic worlds, in part created by technological imagery.

Cinema has always recorded the most varied forms of bodily adherence to utopian worlds. The *Star Wars* saga, for example, through the use of costume and grotesque body imagery, stages an 'inter-ethnic' and 'intergalactic' mix of creatures and humans, which in the narrative finds a meeting point in Moss Healey's inn. The shadowy metropolis in *Blade Runner* is populated by humans and replicants, one of whom, the film's main female character, makes her first appearance dressed in black leather with exaggeratedly wide shoulders, like a 'flesh-and-blood' micro-chip citation of the mechanical creature in *Metropolis*.

What science fiction films have accustomed us to is the equivalent in film imagery of today's hybrid reality. This reality is accurately represented in all those films dealing with subjects like emigration and the relation between 'minorities' and an 'élite', both in the big cities and in the peripheries. *Mississippi Masala* by the Indian director Myra Nair, for example, tells the story of an Indian family who had previously lived in Uganda, but had been forced to emigrate to America, where we witness the contrast between the young daughter – who has completely assimilated the 'habits' of American youth and who falls in love with a 'black' boy – and the older, more traditional women in their saris.

In the 1960s *Caroselli*[1] artificial fibres made up the inventory of shirts, slips and chaste white underwear in the age of the Italian economic boom. Nylon, terital, dacron: the artificial led us to believe in lower prices, less effort while ironing, garments that looked to the future and explicitly alluded to the national and international boom of the chemical industry.

And whoever would have suspected the less than total 'cleanliness' from this industry, in every sense of the word?

A far-off memory, a naïve enthusiasm for a market smelling of poly-amides, is today obscured by a mistrust towards anything which, in one way or another, harms our average concept of 'natural'. Today, in fashion discourse, habits rooted in materials made of synthetic fibres are in crisis in the name of ecology. Designers, fashion houses and 'committed' models have heralded the dawn of an age of 'natural' fabrics, especially cashmere, cotton, velvet, silk and wool, all fabrics that never really disappeared from everyday wear, in any case.[2]

Natural dyeing processes are becoming more and more popular, as it has been proven that dyeing is one of the most polluting phases in the produc-tion of fabrics, because of the harmful residues, which are usually elimi-nated in sewage water. Natural colours, like those used by an Italian hosiery company, are taken from the hull and leaves of nuts, or from a Central American shrub; brazil nut buttons, necklaces made of hazelnuts and almond husks: today ecology becomes fashion.

Prices are obviously very high in *haute couture* ecology. In more wide-spread and everyday fashion consumption, however, the ecological direction has been followed for some time, even though the resonance created by high-profile advertising, which is typical of institutional fashion, is missing. Particularly since our markets have opened their doors to textile production from Asia (countries like Bangladesh, Taiwan, Malaysia, India, Singapore and China), oriental silks and cottons have been adapted to western-style clothing; perhaps not very refined in their cut and style, but attractive all the same for their low prices. Yet such prices also denounce the low cost of manual labour in these countries, which is notoriously exploited by western fashion houses. The long working hours and appalling living conditions of these workers could hardly be deemed 'ecological'!

A textile is a text, one of the texts of which our clothing imagery is made: just as the metaphorical weave gives life to a text – in the common sense of the word, whether written or oral – so the weave of a textile is what gives it a plot, a narrative, which exist thanks to the contact of the textile on the body. Perhaps it is the tactile, tangible dimension of textiles that leads us to reflect on how important it is to rid this contact of a produc-tion that has largely destroyed the relation between human beings and nature. Perhaps our body continues to hide a secret reserve somewhere, a reserve that resists dehumanization, and in asking for natural contact we are probably implicitly alluding to this need to resist, without even real-izing it, as when we enjoy a walk in the mountains or a swim in an unpol-luted sea. And perhaps it is here that fashion discourse meets a less conventional discourse, a sensibility that public communication does not know how to translate.

Amongst those childhood memories that leave a mark because they concern the construction of a clothing image in relation to one's gender, the memory of the fur coat and its role in the so-called 'opulent society' of the 1960s is for me one of the most vivid. I particularly remember a fur coat *manqueé*, my mother's, who like other women of her generation dreamt of having 'a mink before you're forty'. For, as Hollywood films like *How to Marry a Millionaire* taught us, the mink was for the woman who had 'arrived', unless you were among the lucky few who, at twenty-five, could afford a whole coat, not of mink, but of beaver or even ultra-sophisticated leopard. In my house the mink was missing, however, mainly because lower middle-class families at that time thought it was more useful to spend their savings on buying a house, rather than wasting them on a fur coat. Through my youthful eyes the argument for having a new coat made of fabric every two or three years, rather than keeping a single fur coat for life, seemed much more convincing, no matter how seductive the fur coat might have seemed to me.

When my generation was young, no one thought it hypocritical to be friends with animals and yet have a mother at home with a fur coat. Nevertheless, it was well known, especially in Southern Italy, where the thermometer almost never hit zero, that the fur coat was a status symbol, not a necessity, and that the higher one went up the social scale the greater the number of fur coats, jackets and stoles crowded into wardrobes, not to mention the boas that winked eerily through the hangers, giving the impression that the animal was there ready to wrap itself round the unlucky owner's neck.

At Sant'Ambrogio in 1968, for the opening of *La Scala* in Milan, and then at *La Bussola* in Viareggio, the minks, leopards and ermines paraded on the bourgeoisie were targeted by protesting students and the fur coat became the negative symbol *par excellence* of its owner's social status. In the early 1970s young hippies discovered Afghan jackets, smelling of oriental pastures, and wore them over long dresses made of Indian cotton, whilst swaying to the music of the sitar. Or perhaps they dug around in their grandmothers' trunks or at second-hand markets and found old monkey boleros or 'balding' stoles to wear over jeans.

This anti-fashion did not stop the fur industry, however. On the contrary, in the 1970s it joined the designer fashion industry. Soldano, Fendi, Tivioli – to name just a few of the Italian companies – launched the *prêt-à-porter* animal, using styles, models and inventions which until then had been the exclusive property of *haute couture* artisans. Most buyers of fur coats,

however, were then, and still are today, loyal to the small, trusted manu-
facturer, and the role of handmade production (as opposed to industrial
production) is still more substantial here than in any other clothing sector.
The furrier is still trusted today, both because clients wish to follow the
production of a garment from start to finish and because a fur coat is still
an item which, for the average customer, will have to last and will thus
need to be adjusted and altered as the body changes shape. Only a skilled
artisan can guarantee such long-term service.

From the 1970s the 'class' protest against the fur coat began to be
accompanied by protest from the animal protection leagues. It became ever
clearer that, as in other sectors, the relation between the production of
goods and the conservation of nature and its equilibrium was getting out
of control. If people in the coldest parts of the world had been able to wear
fur coats for centuries without endangering the survival of animal species,
mass production, for a market not motivated solely by necessity, put at risk
the lives of species on the brink of extinction, if not already extinct. There
are places where a fur coat is by no means a luxury, but simply a climatic
necessity that padded jackets or 'ecological' furs can substitute only up to
a point. The absurdity of our times is that the indiscriminate slaughter of
animals has upset an equilibrium which had existed in such places for
thousands of years.

There are laws and international conventions that protect certain wild
animals from being hunted, and this has enabled some species to recover;
however, it is well known that poaching is widespread, especially in countries whose economy is traditionally based on the exportation of furs.
Fendi and other designers are always telling us that their furs come exclusively from fur farms, but this argument, albeit true and well documented,
seems less and less sufficient to convince us that fur coats are 'harmless'.
Even some models have refused to wear furs, thereby lending support to
the moral of that famous advertisement in which a fashion show exhibiting
furs is transformed into a blood bath.

There is no doubt that the once popular dream of having 'a mink on
your skin' must today measure itself against the current perception that
this wave of blood is a reality, not just a theatrical scene. Some indication
of a change in mentality can be seen in the increase in sales of classic wool
coats and jackets padded with goose down or made of synthetic leather.
Even sheepskins are an issue for the radically pro-animal organizations:
sheep might not be wild or on the brink of extinction, but they are animals
nonetheless!

At the first sign of winter the first furs (fewer and fewer today) appear
on the streets of a warm Italy: a ritual garment in the wardrobes of elderly

ladies, who would not know what to do without one. The symbol of an ephemeral economic boom, in times of easy money, or a garment worn with conviction at any age and without excuses? In order to be completely loyal to the pro-animal dictum, we should no longer wear leather shoes, bags, or even the much loved leather biker jacket. But the war against fur coats is a war which makes distinctions, with intelligence and without fundamentalism. Above all, it is a symbolic war, articulated around an exemplary 'anti-fur' discourse, in which direct action joins education, including that of little girls, to whom the elderly ladies of today perhaps ought not to pass on their dreams of a mink coat, but rather a framed photograph of a beautiful live mink, running wild in the forest.

Notes

1. A popular advertising television programme in Italy in the 1960s.

2. Among the artificial fabrics that seem to have been saved from 'naturalist' propaganda is viscose, a fibre of natural origins that comes from wood pulp and is widely used for linings, sweaters, suits, blouses and leisure clothing. Rayon viscose, invented in England at the end of the nineteenth century and in widespread use after the Second World War, is perhaps the best known.

Fashion and Cinema

9

At the beginning of the 1960s Barthes wrote that cinema had become 'a model means of mass communication' (Barthes (1998: 41). Today this statement is still valid, since the representation of the visible offered by cinema, constructed by the camera lens as if it were reality before our very eyes, communicated and reproduced in millions of copies, is unique and irreplaceable. Thinking through images is equivalent to representing the real; the metaphors and narratives in cinema have become an integral part of our daily lives. Verisimilitude in film is the 'truth' that fuels our imagination. Cinema 'thinks': it invents stories, narrative techniques, human types and bodily forms; it explores territories at the limits of experience, feelings and passions from the most banal to the most eccentric.

The human subjects that cinema makes visible inhabit our world as persistent icons. They are the stars, the divas of Hollywood, the characters who have marked an age or a dream, and who can transform themselves into wayfarers of the everyday. In order to be such – whether in reality or fantasy – these characters must circumscribe their space with concrete signs: dress, makeup, hairstyles are the main ones, those which construct a character beginning with his/her physical appearance.

In that makeshift station of life called reality, no one, not even the most distracted person, can say in all sincerity that they put on the first thing that comes to hand. Getting dressed, even casually, fixing our hair, putting on makeup, etc., is a language that always 'recounts' something. Even more so in cinema, where every sign on the body of a character has a precise meaning, linked to social characterization, historical identity, grotesque emphasis, transformation in terms of personality or feeling, and so on. Thus in the great sense-making machine of cinema, costume represents yet another signifying system, the signs of which become distinctive features, functioning as linguistic units that are often more important than script or sound track.[1]

If vision is to support thought, if it is to help structure belief, then it must be anchored in signs, like costumes in film that make the text more coherent, or at times speak in place of movement and dialogue. Verisimilitude in cinema has been defined as that which concerns the relation of a text to public opinion, and its relation to other texts, but also the internal functioning of the story it recounts (Aumont *et al.* 1994). Verisimilitude thus doesn't concern just realistic cinema (the degree of adhesion to the historical, spatial and social reality represented), but a more complex resonance between cultural texts, including current public opinion that cinema itself helps to construct and certainly to cement. What we call 'received meaning' falls into this category of opinion.[2]

The image of the cowboy, for instance, in its appearance style (see Kaiser 1992) in the classic Western: the dusters around the legs, the ten-gallon hat, the fringed jacket and trousers, the holster with pistol, an essential prosthesis in the representation of this type. Just how much realism do these images contain? Is there any similarity between John Wayne and an 'authentic' nineteenth century photo portrait of a gunman in the Wild West? The answer is that what counts is not so much the adhesion of the clothed body in the film to a model established by the 'real' (which is itself only a construction of the photographer's studio), but the degree of verisimilitude that the signs on the body manage to define and the 'veridiction contract' (see Greimas 1983) drawn up between the film and its viewers. This 'veridiction contract' is a sort of implicit accord between the two parties, or agents, in the communication process, sender and receiver, which are not necessarily two physical people, but rather two positions, or figures, in a discourse. A character's clothes, accessories or hairstyle in a costume drama may appear verisimilar to the viewer if the latter's encyclopaedia contains prior knowledge of the apparel in vogue during the historical period in which the film is set[3] and, moreover, if the images manage to make that costume credible at a textual and intertextual level, if they manage to stimulate the viewers' imagination (as a semiotic activity productive of other worlds).[4]

Thus in the contract tacitly drawn up between the polyphonic complexity (director, cast, film industry, etc.) of the film discourse and the multilayered social subject, only reductively called 'the public' or 'viewers', *verisimilitude* is transformed into *veridiction*. The terms of the contract concern the fact that not only is the clothed body on the screen credible, it is also socially 'true' and that one can recreate from its image other like bodies, not only in film, but in reality, whether past or present.

Costume drama is film in historical costume, but what about cinema that represents the present or the future, fleeting forms of time that the twentieth century (the century of cinema) has invented to recount and imagine itself. Here cinema encounters that other great modelling system of communication, fashion. Cinema manages to act beyond the limits of image and representation, penetrating the ways in which clothed bodies think and reproduce themselves through fashion as a great syntax, or better, as a system of writing, inscription and presentation of the body to the world. If the film 'brings fashion with it', recording tastes and trends of the moment, then it is also true that in virtue of the strange resonance between vision, veridiction and fantasy, cinema manages to anticipate and orient these tastes and trends, creating prototypes and styles. We might call this a movement from the social to the filmic and vice versa.

Cinema and fashion: two institutions, two sign systems, two languages that pose the problem of the relation between image and identity. From the visual identity of the moving image to the bodily identity of everyday life, and between the two the question of how we think, dream and imagine ourselves. Jacques Aumont (1994) attributes to cinema an inventive capacity that often manifests itself not only at the level of narration, but also at the level of form and plasticity of image, and of human representation. This inventive capacity, continues Aumont, often manifests itself in seemingly insignificant elements, which are nevertheless essential from the viewpoint of the film's reception, that is, from the viewpoint of someone who perhaps isn't even aware of their importance, yet benefits from the effects of their meaning.

Filmic representation literally constructs a world in which social subjects are depicted in relation to one other. The cinema is a sense-making machine that produces feelings, sensations and desires. Often clothes are mediators in this 'sense-making', not as mere objects, but as signs charged with social significance that the camera gaze, associated with the viewer's gaze, reinvents and thus restores to everyday semantic practices.

As examples of this, lets look at two scenes from two Hollywood classics. In *Double Indemnity* the female character, played by Barbara Stanwyck, is seen for the first time by the male character as she descends the stairs with a bracelet jingling at her ankle. The viewers see her legs appear to the rhythm of this jingle from the male character's viewpoint, which is also the viewpoint of the camera lens. The other scene is from *Gilda*, when the eponymous heroine dances and sings as she takes off her long gloves under the attentive gaze of a room full of spectators, and of her male partner, whose viewpoint coincides with that of the camera and so with ours. In both cases, the movie camera publicly and socially represents desire through the male gaze, a gaze which is proposed as 'natural', 'objective' and pleasurably shared by men and women alike as a 'neutral' form of representation.

In *Notorious*, on the other hand, Hitchcock frames a possible object of female desire: the back of Cary Grant's neck, who is filmed from behind when he appears for the first time in Ingrid Bergman's house. The difference here, with regard to the other two examples, is that we see him from behind (and for quite a long time) as he stands in front of Ingrid Bergman, and so the gaze of the female character, the public's gaze and the viewpoint of the camera do not coincide, do not create a natural and objective effect of 'universality'. The female viewer can, if she likes, concentrate her desire on the actor's neck in a starched white collar, but hers will be a 'particular', not a 'universal', gaze.

Thus, the male or female body 'written' by clothes and seen through the camera lens is already part of a network of socio-sexual relations that define it, but it also directs these definitions to the reality outside the film, sometimes as stereotype, sometimes as irony, excess and cross-evaluation. In *L'homme qui aimait les femmes*, by François Truffaut, for example, the relation between the camera eye and the male gaze is treated with meta-semiotic irony, expressed in the repeated and obsessive construction of female corporeality through the male character-voyeur's favourite bit of the woman: her legs in smooth silk stockings.

Every time we watch a film our mind's eye sees the fashions depicted in it as an essential, yet barely perceptible message that is transmitted as 'natural'. We have learnt from Barthes (1957) that the transformation of culture into nature is at the basis of the 'linguistic theft' of contemporary myth. Cinema and fashion are two great reservoirs of myths, cults and stars: we dream of being Audrey Hepburn standing in front of Tiffany's in her little Givenchy number; we are inspired in our choice of leather jacket by a 'wild' Marlon Brando; we feel the pain of Anna Magnani in neo-real-istic black. And even more recently, we imagine that we too can have blue hair like Stefania Rocca in *Nirvana*, the Gaultier outfits in *The Fifth Element*, or the wrist gadgets in *To the End of the World*.

And yet fashion and cinema manage to restore reflections on myth to the social sphere, using at times paradoxical techniques. For example, assigning to an item of clothing a performative function that creates a sort of symbolic disorder, as in William Wyler's *Jezebel*, where the red dress worn by the female character (Bette Davis) represents a challenge to social convention. Disguise and transvestism are further techniques that can become crucial to the film's narration, as in *Victor/Victoria* where a woman dressed as a man then pretends to be a man dressed as a woman. Or nudity in *The Full Monty*, where the parodied male striptease becomes an ironic strategy of social resistance and the redefinition of sexual roles.

Ugo Volli (1998: 96) writes that between fashion and cinema there is a relation of competition, contamination and complicity, three almost 'pas-sionate' conditions uniting two sign systems that explicitly cite one another, albeit with different results and to different effect. Emblematic of this is Antonioni's film *Blow Up*, in which the world of fashion acts as a backdrop both to a narration of slight importance and to the problem of the truth-status of images. A transgenerational aura has been created around this film, based partly on David Hemmings' models, like Verushka, whose names and bodies constructed the worldly image of the pop model typical of fashion as a form of popular culture (see Calefato 1996), partly on the atmosphere of Swinging London as an ideal, metropolitan space for a revolution in dress (experienced as such by later generations, too), and partly on the construction of new and original images of women, like Vanessa Redgrave and Jane Birkin, who didn't conform to stereotypes and yet were radiantly beautiful.

The same aura doesn't surround Robert Altman's rather cold film *Prêt-à-Porter* in which the director has dryly presented the glossy world of 1980s fashion as an obscene freak-show of vacuous stereotypes. The fashion-parade of nude models is exemplary of this and makes evident the director's idea that institutional fashion has completed exhausted its inventive capacity and so only shock techniques (the total cancellation of signs) are left to it; and that, moreover, the public will accept anything presented to it on the catwalk, including messages that are completely devoid (or denuded) of sense, as in Hans Christian Andersen's tale *The Emperor's New Clothes*.

As communication systems, fashion and cinema are joined together by a unique synergy; their relation cannot be adequately defined by simply recalling cult images, and any analysis must include the whole polyphony of hands and eyes that go to producing both. The role of the costume designer[5] is an essential part of this polyphony. The work of the costume designer and that of the fashion designer are certainly different, even though at times it is the fashion designer who not only creates the costumes for a film, but also decides their function as a semiotic unit within the film's narration. Jean Paul Gaultier's role in *The Fifth Element* is exemplary of this (just as Moebius' is for the architecture) and differs in kind from Givenchy's role, for example, in films starring Audrey Hepburn, since in the latter case the 'tailor' himself designed the star's body, whereas in the former the complex institutions of fashion and architecture in their entirety are the image-makers, becoming narrative and stylistic units in themselves.

Renata Molho (1998) writes that the fashion designer's only constraint is the body, while the costume designer must take into account pre-defined factors and technical means. The fashion designer can, however, enter a film 'metasemiotically' as in the exhibition at the 1998 *Biennale di Firenze* dedicated to the relation between fashion and cinema, where nine fashion designers were each invited to rework a scene, a theme or a significant moment from one of nine Italian films.[6] In the same exhibition, in the space dedicated to *Cine-Moda*, seven films from the 1990s were cited as instrumental in revolutionizing the relation between fashion and cinema; a revolution that heralded the return of the 'style film' (see Martin & Wilkes 1998) in which costume, objects and style have a central role and share, sometimes even usurp, the limelight with plot and actors.

What remains of all this apart from the image on the screen? Garments from famous films are venerated and exhibited as icons or auctioned at astronomical prices: the grandiose caparisons of *The Last Emperor*, the red velvet dress with a minute waist worn by Michele Pfeiffer in *The Age of Innocence,* the magical twinkling shoe by Ferragamo in Andy Tennant's *A Cinderella Story.* Or else, a style remains, with which to construct a piece of the history of the modern propensity to think through images.[7]

In cinema the central importance of visual signs is indisputable, even though they do not exhaust its complexity of languages, or better, the heterogeneity of cinematic language that goes to make up a film (Aumont *et al.* 1994). In the sign system of fashion, on the other hand, the status of the visual remains to be investigated, and thus speaking of the relation between visual semiotics and fashion becomes a sort of epistemological challenge to the history of twentieth century semiotics, especially Barthes' project of a 'fashion system' conceived essentially as the reduction of the garment to the word, the primacy of linguistics over semiology and of the verbal over the non-verbal. Nearly fifty years after the publication of Barthes' work, semiotics now fully recognizes that it is possible to go beyond this project of 'reading' a garment only within the limits of described fashion; and this lesson has been learnt from Barthes himself! As Gianfranco Marrone writes, fashion was for Barthes 'a type of discourse in which clothing practices, aesthetic representations and specialized utterances merged in a complex *life form*' (Marrone 1998). Just as fashion is not merely the word, nor is it merely the image, even though its grip on the world comes about primarily through a visual dimension. This dimension concerns the semiotics of the styles, forms and materials of which fashion garments are made, as well as the function of fashion as a mediator between taste and received meaning, a mediation which is realized through the special relation fashion sets up between signs, sense perceptions and social discourses.

Before continuing, however, I would like to clarify a few concepts. Primarily that of the 'clothed body' as a semiotic category epitomizing the ways in which, through its visual dimension, the subject establishes its being in the world and its appearance style (see Calefato 1986, 1992, 1996). Dressing in this sense is a non-verbal language, a device for modelling the world, a form of projection and simulation, valid for both the individual and society. As transformation along a given line of thought, the semiotics of the clothed body emphasizes, in multifarious forms, the relation between signs and the senses. Through clothing, the body seems to 'feel' the surrounding world in a complete and amplified form. This world may be examined in the light of two semiotic perspectives: as a *continuum*, as amorphous material – 'Hamlet's cloud' Hjelmslev calls it – that language, whether verbal or non-verbal, organizes into meaning; or as a place where there is already a manifestation of the sensible, which then becomes a manifestation of human sense.[8] From both perspectives the relation between the 'world' and these languages is presented in terms of Lévi-Strauss' image of a *bricolage*. In anthropological terms, *bricolage* is the art of linking objects and signs that are seemingly devoid of a reciprocal connection, yet whose sequence, or collection, is presented as a cognate system with respect to the so-called 'natural' world. This sense-producing art gives rise to what we might define as a network of correlations between different levels of signifying reality, each having their own sense qualities. The clothed body articulates what the world still doesn't know, feel or possess, if we adopt the metaphor of 'Hamlet's cloud'. Or it can feel in a more exciting, tense and 'hip' form – to use musical jargon – what the world already feels, if we adopt Greimas' proposition of a world pervaded by *aesthesia* and sensorial receptivity, which is above all *synaesthesia*, the potential of the senses to interact, combine with or even substitute one another.

In traditional societies, dressing, masquerading, tattooing, adorning, in other words 'covering' the body, are regulated by a sociocultural syntax we call 'costume'. In the context of the social reproduction of modernity, and even more so in our age of mass reproduction, this sociocultural syntax is determined by 'fashion'. Today fashion is a sign system that fully manifests itself as a system of mass communication, as daily dressing up, as a form of popular culture, as worldliness and 'mass fashion' able to reinvent and reproduce itself constantly, through its interaction with other languages too. Given this status, fashion is a system that governs and produces forms of perception and bodily sensation connected with the need for social approval. Today, however, such social approval only partially concerns what was for Simmel the 'reassuring' nature of fashion, adherence to which would not compromise the territory of the individual spirit. Now that the sign system of fashion covers myriad aspects, including its potential for mass reproduction in serial form, the relation between fashion and sensorial experience is becoming ever more complex: the notion of 'feeling' the world through fashion is now fundamental to an understanding of its social dimension, as well as of its semiotic modes of production and communication.

The two above-mentioned theoretical approaches – one in which the various human languages make sense of a 'mute' world, the other in which human languages appropriate sense elements already in the natural world – are really parallel, one impling the other, even though academically they are seen as distinct and separate. If, indeed, there is a sense 'of the world' in the language of fashion, today this consists in 'giving the word' to a sentient world, which is nevertheless mute with regard to the unheard, the unexpected and the non-stereotypical. A world in which, as Baudelaire writes, merging with the crowd – the highest aspiration of his 'painter of modern life' – means recognizing, too, that the crowd can be a 'human desert'.

Not the fashion system in its solemn, institutional, reassuring and élite version, but rather a felt, lived and rhythmic dimension within everyday contexts that are permeated by a *synaesthesic* tension. Fashion anticipates moments of transition and distils transformations in taste. Even the relation between taste and style can be collocated in the topsy-turvy image of the carnivalesque semantic inversion of the grotesque body, which is the true 'subject' of non-institutional and worldly fashion. The clothed body as a disguised body – as a play between irony, harmony and dissonance – is grotesque and is the focal point of an inverted aesthetic quest.

In this context, the concept of 'body writing' in clothing has a fundamental role as a concept freed from its exclusive dependency on the verbal. Writing both as non-sequential, non-alphabetical syntax, as hypertextual syntax articulating the 'collection' of signs on the clothed body, and as sense perception connected to the individual and social gesture of clothing the body. Just as any other medium, new or old, just as any other visual form, fashion is imbued with social practices that the techniques of simulation in stylistic creation, reproduction and execution have introduced in the production of discourses and identities. Thus on the contemporary scene, writing and simulacrum (see Talens 1994) intersect, clash and coincide: the imagery of the clothed body is produced through intertextual strategies supported by various sign and communications systems, from photography, to specialized journalism, music, metropolitan culture, computer science, design, audio-visual systems and, last but not least, cinema.

Today cinema, in particular, represents one of the most complete and multifarious universes of social imagery, and has a more relevant role in relation to fashion than photography even, since it empowers human sensibility through the complexity of signs, discourses and forms of perception that it triggers. Fashion and cinema are two forms of the visible, two social discourses concerned with style, form and execution in terms of their materials, and with time, space and the body in terms of their content, use and 'uniform' as institutions.

A film that may be considered as a significant, unconventional example of the relation between vision and writing, and of the simultaneous and *synaesthesic* sense-making processes of both fashion and cinema is Wim Wenders' *Aufzeichnungen zu Kleidern und Städten*, a kind of poetic interview with fashion designer Yohji Yamamoto, who speaks of the dual, synergetic creative processes of cinema and fashion, two media at the heart of the metropolitan scene.

Wenders' film came out in 1989: the end of the 1980s was the time when the reproducible arts definitively substituted representation with simulation. The binary relation between the 'thing' and the sign that represents it – for example, between the film-negative and the scene represented analogically – was substituted by the *synthetic* construction of the thing, its direct creation through the smallest impulses and units of digital information. The central question with which the film opens is thus a question about the relation between image and identity.

The film opens with a running text of Wenders' reflections on the concept of identity: 'Identity ... what is identity? To know where you belong? To know what you are worth? To know who you are? We create an image of ourselves, we attempt to resemble that image. Is that what we call identity: the accord between the image we have created of ourselves and ... ourselves?'

From the alternating eye of film and video camera – framing an angle of the transparent corridors of the Pompidou Centre dominating the Paris skyline, or the Grande Arche from Neuilly Cemetery – and with frequent recourse to a kind of montage somewhere between digital and analogical, so that Yamamoto's face is often duplicated within the main frame on a small video screen, Wenders embarks on an unexpected and unusual voyage through fashion as a contemporary form of popular culture. The director's voice-over makes an ingenuous remark at the beginning: 'I'm interested in the world, not in fashion,' said as a sort of self-defence against the film's project of *Fashion and the City* commissioned by the Pompidou Centre. And yet, three projects are implicitly contained in this remark: the film, the city and fashion. Fashion, the world and the metropolis have become one thing, the emblem, metaphor and *élan vital* of which is *the image*, especially the electronic image, the image reproduced by the video camera that Wenders uses for filming the city, or rather bringing the city to life. Cinema is fashion, fashion is the city, the city is the world: 'We live in cities, cities live in us. Time passes, we move from one city to another, we change languages, we change habits, we change opinions, we change clothes.'

The film could also be interpreted as a revisitation à la Baudelaire and Benjamin of Paris as a twenty-first century capital.[9] World-city, fashion-city, a city built on imagery that is both technological and nostalgic, the metropolis contains both the present and the past-in-the-present, as in the lingering shots of old bridges over the Seine interspersed with images of Paris at the end of the millennium. This city is also the *sine qua non* for the potential existence of every other metropolis, the confirmation of the planetary city – a bit Paris, a bit Tokyo, Los Angeles and Berlin – as it appears in *Bis ans Ende der Welt*.

Fashion circulates the body, and the city is its favourite backdrop, for it is here that the *flâneurs* and *flâneuses* of signs move in a continuous passage of desire, identity and relations. The mater-polis, the mother city, embraces all that is haphazard, anonymous, reproducible, multicultural, and a fragmented, multiple, masked identity, while at the same time creating an illusion of absolute originality and exclusiveness in every gesture exhibited, every pose assumed and every garment worn.

Both Yamamoto and Wenders love the confusion of the city; both feel that urban identity is a question of image, of identity in and with the crowd. Urban identity is 'being for others', the sense of which, linked to fetishism in forms of bodily representation as perceived by Benjamin, both film director and fashion designer have completely and passionately embraced, as emerges from their dialogue. Artificers of two different creative processes, in their respective occupations, they seek a coexistence between inventiveness and memory, which may even take the form of a contrast, or chiasmus, between two tensions. While he is talking, Yamamoto leafs through a book of old portrait photographs by Auguste Sander: faces of men and women in their working gear, bodies whose social role is recognizable in their clothes, linked to a given task, to a temporal scansion of the day, and of life. The metropolis deprives the garment of this function, theoretically close to pure, essential form; it deprives bodies of their identification. From profoundly *within* metropolitan culture, and with the mature awareness of a distant memory, yet without any sense of nostalgia, the designer focuses his energy on recovering this essence, this form.

'To find the essence of a thing in the production process.' Yamamoto's remark reveals his commitment to finding a sensorial identity for form and body through the production and manufacture (including manual work) of a garment. In his commentary Wenders says that he became curious about Yamamoto's fashion when he saw its effect on Solveig Dommartin: 'Dressed like that she seemed transformed every time, as if those garments gave her body a new role' (Wenders 1998: 77).

The film shows the designer making a dress to measure directly on a model's body. As if he were writing on the woman's body, the designer stands back to get a better look, then goes up to take the measurements.

On each wrist is tied a pincushion, which he uses throughout the session, constantly manipulating, cutting, tearing, folding and pinning the garment on the model. Near him lies a book of old photographs in which there is one of a Japanese woman in a kimono. As in some ancient dress ritual, in which the woman covers her body with the kimono, tying it at the waist with an *obi*, the fitting session is a way of discovering the pure gesture of dressing and of the garment as the essence, the absolute form of this gesture.

Yamamoto does not like being called a Japanese designer, part of a class, a group. And yet he *is* Japan within Europe and beyond; Japan as the 'country of writing' (so Barthes defined it). Yamamoto's garments are pure form; like the Japanese haiku, they are 'a brief event that suddenly finds its exact form' (Barthes 1984: 88).

Thus the colour he most prefers is black, since it exhibits the body essentially as a silhouette, as 'sign and symbol, totem and message' (Barthes 1982: 114). His forms are rigorously asymmetrical: symmetry says Yamamoto 'isn't human'. Nor are those pointed shoes with stiletto heels that western woman love to wear, but which the designer totally bans from his female outfits, using instead shoes which are flat, silent, essential. Symmetry is not human: the 'touch', as Yamamoto calls it, comes first; it achieves a notion of the present as a tension that does not seek harmony, but imperfection, the detail that jars, will not stay in place, and so enhances meaning. Yet, as we know, that *is* its place, in a different order. The gaze knows where to look, the eyes seek to touch, to amplify the senses in that special form of creativity – quest and discovery – which is the process itself of creation and through which one can 'sense the sensible'.

Looking at a photograph of Jean Paul Sartre by Cartier Bresson, the designer is struck by an apparently insignificant detail that actually distils meaning for him, a *punctum* Barthes would call it: the coat collar. The collar tells him that the overcoat was Sartre's friend, in all its simplicity. For Yamamoto, fashion, especially male fashion, seeks a simplicity like that of Sartre's overcoat, a simplicity in which fabric and form communicate across two different languages.

Simplicity lies in the search for a creative process that produces real, essential things: chairs, shirts, overcoats ... The 'real' garment, the simple things are concerned with life, while consumerism is the exact opposite, says Yamamoto. And Wenders comments: 'After a while I thought I had discovered a paradox in Yohji's work: what he produced was necessarily ephemeral, slave to the immediate and rapacious consumption imposed by fashion as one of the rules of the game. What counts is only the *here* and *now*, not yesterday. Nevertheless, Yohji could find inspiration in an old photo, in period clothes, from workers who lived to a different rhythm and who found in work a different dignity. So Yohji seemed to me to express himself simultaneously in two languages, to play two different instruments at the same time: one ephemeral, the other permanent, one fleeting, the other enduring, one mutable, the other immutable' (Wenders 1998: 77–8).[10]

The 'sex appeal of merchandise' exhibited by fashion finds its carnivalesque overturning in Yamamoto's project: for the designer, fashion should 'take us home', help us rediscover a familiar friend. Fashion should substitute *unheimlich* (the unfamiliar) with *heimlich* (the familiar), following the perverse mechanism identified by Freud, on the basis of which the most familiar things become strange and disturbing. Today more than ever our 'home' is part of this estrangement.

The designer's work consists in representing time: 'you design time,' says Yamamoto. His work, like the director's, competes with consumption and wear-and-tear. And so the joint project of cinema and fashion might be conceived as one of comprehending fully the human tension towards the past within the present.

Wenders lingers over the designer's and his assistants' hands as they work on various fashion projects; hands at work replicated by the electronic eye in their unique and infinite movements, attitudes, hesitations. The hands are workers, generating products and artefacts; their activity is an isotope of the 'manipulation' of the camera-eye. Yet again, fashion and cinema are intrinsically linked in their triggering of *synaesthesic* generative processes. The director reveals such processes when, for example, he projects an image simultaneously onto two different screens, the traditional cinema screen and the digital video screen in miniature, another Japanese 'prodigy', at once the dream of a Lilliputian shrinking of the world and the new panopticon of that world. The filmic 'writing' takes on a hypertextual, non-linear dimension: the video inside the screen opens like a window and recalls a link in a narrative time chain.

The relation between manual skill and writing (here using the alphabet) is explored in the filming of Yamamoto's repeated attempts to write his signature on the signboard of his new Tokyo emporium. This continual rehearsal is carried out, not with a copy, but with the real thing, the designer's signature, the metonym hovering between the designer's body and his work.

The proper name, the trademark, the designer label are elements of language that can tell stories, invent worlds and produce signs that transcend the universe of words. All the graphological components of writing are epitomized in the designer's name, or rather in his signature (see Calefato

1992b). These components fluctuate between the search for a correspondence between hand and signature – that is, the search for an identity – and the transformation of the garment into a pure sign.

The final moment of the project, what the designer's hands have worked towards, is the *défilé*, though it is not a *finale* conceived as a temporal sequence, nor as the film's happy ending in terms of classic narrative closure. Just as the film shows its technical approaches to work (for example, the director's reflections on the use of film and video cameras) and is not proffered as final or definitive, so the *défilé* of Yamamoto's models in front of the Louvre Pyramid is presented and represented through all its rehearsals and preparations; even its 'final draft' (a phrase used metaphorically, as if the *défilé* were a book) is seen obliquely through simultaneous visual windows.

The Wenders-Yamamoto *défilé* is not presented like those we normally see on television, with their sleek catwalks, fodder for even the most trivial, commercial entertainment industries, where identical bodies and garments seem like serialized transcriptions. Instead the *défilé* is seen as a fashion-representation machine, as writing, as a text organized down to the smallest detail, as a backstage where a team of form-manipulators have worked as if in a monastery (says Wenders). Promenading on the catwalk is like promenading on the street, when on the sidewalk of a crowded city street we try to focus on a body, a face, a garment, or a silhouette, through its apparition in the myriad forms of the crowd. 'Everything is a copy,' says Wenders at the beginning, 'I saw the group before me as if it were a cinema troupe, and Yohji in the middle was the director of a film without end' (Wenders 1998: 83).

There is a direct, fixed gaze, a stare that recalls the identity and order of discourse, and through which you 'say things straight'. Lacan calls it a gaze that arrests life; it is the *evil eye*. And there is also a distracted, indirect and mobile gaze that brings things together in space and time, while simultaneously making them blurred and distant. This gaze also gives value to the insignificant. As Benjamin has shown, photography and cinema make such mobility and distraction of the gaze possible. Photography, because it *contains* all reality and doesn't allow the gaze the privilege of selection and hierarchy in representation and because, in it, automatism and memory are indissolubly linked. Cinema, because it is concerned by definition with the movement of the gaze in search of the other, be it simply (this 'other') realistic representation. In its movement, cinema is close to fashion, itself an art of movement: 'There isn't just a fashion of clothes, there's also a fashion of buildings, cars, rock music, watches, books and films … Fashion is also movement, and perhaps herein lies its true function' (Wenders 1998: 82).

Since cinema, like fashion, mobilizes the gaze, inviting it to change, to transform, it can narrate these metamorphoses, can narrate itself and display the cultural and technical processes that generate meaning. In cinema, vision encounters the other senses, and so the pleasure induced by the film is a *synaesthesic* pleasure in which the senses become confused and the viewer is initiated to an unfamiliar visual pleasure based on a mutual contamination of the senses. In the most elementary act of perception the senses are not subject to a hierarchy, whereas in our world the primacy of sight and seeing (as the direct, fixed gaze, Lacan's *evil eye*) has made us forget all the rest, all the *synaestheses* and possible distractions from the visible.

The questions posed by Wenders about fashion directly concern vision as representation, as a copy through which images *think for us* and through which the sacred aura of the mass-produced, serialized work that accompanies contemporary mythology (*pace* Benjamin) is constructed. Fashion, too, has this aura, which makes it difficult to speak of fashion as myth *tout court*, though in everyday language, when we refer to myth and the mythical, it is the discourses of fashion and cinema that seem best to fit such a definition. The star system in cinema corresponds to the top model in fashion, and both discourses have to do with a system of objects with which the body is clothed, whether in real or imaginary form. Think of all the gadgets that come out with every new Disney movie, the T-shirts with lines from famous films on them (from *Casablanca* to *Dear Diary*), and the futuristic technological objects in films like *To the End of the World*. This mythical aura seems to surround not only cinema and fashion, but also what we (perhaps wrongly?) call 'reality'. One such instance of 'the real' is death: the myth of film stars untimely ripped from life (for example, James Dean and Brandon Lee) is repeated, albeit in a more solemn and sophisticated form, in the myths of Gianni Versace and Moschino, whose memories are almost hallowed, whether it be in the recognition of artistic quality, as in the case of Versace, or in the survival of a name in support of humanitarian causes, as in the case of Moschino with Aids.

Actually, in fashion and cinema, rather than *myth* as a closed system, we are dealing with *the mythical* in the various social discourses through which both systems are articulated. We are also dealing with widespread intersemiotic practices, on the basis of which an image is directly measured against corporeality, with its being presentation rather than representation; that is, the way in which the body gives itself to the world as worked material, style, sense-making performance, sign, text and object exposed to unexpected forms of otherness, rather than as replicant closure within an identical form.[11]

Today the imagery of the clothed body is produced through intertextual strategies in which fashion interacts with cinema, photography, journalism, advertising, music, sport, television, metropolitan culture, information technology and design. The construction of the social significance of dress is channelled through these widespread intersemiotic practices that allow the mixing and remixing of styles and tastes, a sort of navigating between signs where one can choose either affiliation or travesty and disguise.

For instance, today the relation between clothes and sport expresses much more than just the simple functional utilisation of an object in specific contexts, much more than just simple changes in fashionable items within sporting contexts. The relation is one of mutual contamination, as we can see by the widespread use of sports clothes (running shoes and track suits, in particular) in contexts devoid of any sporting or athletic reference. Many of these garments (for example, Nike brand items) are emblematic of a certain lifestyle, especially among the younger generations; or, seen from another perspective, they are signs that allow the symbolic eruption of free time in everyday or working environments, as a kind of carnivalesque travesty and disguise. For instance, in the film *Le bonheur est dans les prés* putting on a pair of Nike trainers epitomizes the character's passage of identity, the transformation from heavy to light in his life and in those around him.

Perennial reproducibility in fashion is flanked by clothing practices that seem to echo the daily reinvention of consumption and directly involve unconventional sensorial forms. One of these forms is *vintage* clothing, today a communicative style making explicit the sensuality of wearing used clothes, in which we live and relive our own personal history through that of others. In her novel *L'amant* Marguerite Duras speaks of the narcissistic pleasure felt by the main character when she puts on an old worn-out silk dress that used to belong to her mother. The composition of used 'pieces' becomes an appearance style paradoxically in tune with a new thrift, which does not, however, preclude eccentricity. In this case the traditional mechanism of fashion, through which semiotic wear-and-tear is more important than physical wear-and-tear and defines the rhythms of consumption, is inverted. The second-hand garment (perhaps even with a designer label) enters the communicative circuits of production, exchange and consumption in which veritable temples are erected; the Vintage Palace, for example, in Italy has become a seat of exhibitions and an historical archive of dress consulted by designers and scholars alike, as well as an emporium of clothing signs available to cinema too.

Another aspect of the transformation of a sense dimension into social reproduction is *revival*, a strategy that has always characterized fashion cycles. According to Simmel, revival represents maximum thrift, ironic eternal return, a parody of cyclical time, hovering between parsimony and excess, repetition and waste. The repetitive nature of fashion revival is a caricature of accumulation, a mockery of linear time, and today it manifests itself in the fragmented decontextualization, syncopated like a jazz performance, of signs from the past, which are either adapted to or directly revived in the present. This backward movement in time, a classic law of fashion, carries with it an ethical principle that concerns social subjects more than clothing practices. Looking to the past by dressing in the past is less a fact of fashion, in the institutional sense, and more a fact of sharing fully an experience, as we can see in the history of urban street styles and in the social practice today of the *bricolage* of old and new, and the overlapping of different seasons and styles.

Today fashion and cinema (as well as music and design) have a particular interest in the recent past (twenty-five to thirty years ago), revisited not only in the latest technology, but also in the popular craze for vinyl records. In cinema Quentin Tarantino's film *Jackie Brown* recaptures and recontextualizes both the 1970s 'black' B-movie genre and the body and performance of Pam Grier, an actress of the period. Another device is chiasmus, when the body becomes the arena for a stylistic or formal tension; for example, between nature and artifice (a Punk style), masculine and feminine (a *camp* style; see Colaizzi 1999), or between contrasting styles.

Sensorial investment in an *object*, in this case, concerns the search for that aesthetic moment in-the-balance, strange, experimental and 'felt', rather than uncritical and stereotypical identification with the object-myth. Greimas speaks of the fragment and metonymy as producing *aesthesis*; for example, from the curved line left by a woman's body after she has brushed past a window, not only can we reconstruct her whole body, but also concepts such as elegance and simplicity (Marrone 1995: 53). Writing on the body is a form of metonymy; in this writing, the sign fulfils the visionary desire of revealing meaning before the latter turns into stereotype.

The opposition, the balance, between two extremes, the unexpected, unheard note all produce a particular form of aesthetic pleasure – not necessarily linked to beauty – that turns the body into a place of passage and metamorphosis. In his film on Yamamoto, Wenders speaks of his first encounter with the designer – when he first wore clothes with a Yamamoto label – as a sort of 'encounter with identity':

> I had bought a shirt and jacket. You know the sensation you feel when you put on a new garment: you look in the mirror, happy and a bit excited in your new skin. But wearing that shirt and jacket I was different; they were *old* and *new* at

the same time. In the mirror I was *myself*, undoubtedly, only I was *more myself* than before. I had a strange sensation ... yes, I was wearing *the* shirt par excellence and the perfect jacket, and beneath them I was *myself*. I felt protected, like a knight in his armour. (Wenders 1998: 75–6)

The emotion of dressing as an emotion given by time writing on the body its identity ... The sensorial dimension here becomes a political dimension: perceiving, communicating and dressing can all be forms of resistance to received meaning, while still making *feeling* common currency. This might be a way to utilize fetishism – the living power of objects on and around us – feeling their sensorial being, while rejecting their totalitarianism.

Notes

1. A good example is Visconti's *Il gattopardo* in which the meticulously reconstructed costumes 'speak' throughout the whole film, especially in the ballroom scene, translating the deeper sense of the story into images.
2. Received meaning is to be understood as a totality or aggregate of beliefs and forms of sensibility that are constructed in communication, as the space where social values and meanings are brought together.
3. Often, in the recreation of historical costume, a production studio will turn to pictorial texts for its choice of clothes, hairstyles, objects, fabrics and even gestures typical of a given historical period.
4. In this way, the film transcends the limits of encyclopaedic knowledge.
5. A profession generally practised by women, such as Edith Head in the golden era of Hollywood, or the Oscar-winning Gabriella Pescucci for her costumes in *The Age of Innocence*.
6. *C'era una volta in America, Il giardino dei Finzi-Contini, E la nave va, La decima vittima, Medea, Il gattopardo, Carosello napoletano, Il conformista*.
7. An undertaking as disruptive in its elucidatory force as the invitation from cinema to think no longer in terms of stereotypes.
8. This is a concept used by Greimas.
9. A city in which, like Benjamin's Paris, capital of the twentieth century, fashion is one of the most visible and deeply felt forms of popular urban culture.
10. Thus fashion allows a sort of inter-semiotic translation between different times, different "languages" as Wenders calls them; it can show two different times simultaneously through a technique it certainly shares with cinema.
11. The difference between presentation and representation directly concerns the philosophical problem of the sign as otherness in communication, regardless of the search for the 'truth' of the representation; see Ponzio 1997: 179–80.

10

Wearing Black

In the film *Reservoir Dogs*, Quentin Tarantino alludes unmistakably to the black suit and dark glasses worn by the famous duo in *The Blues Brothers* (see Chapters 3 and 8), though the stylistic features he constructs are inverted with respect to John Landis' film[2]. And paradoxically, the characters, who all wear black, are named after other colours: Mr. White, Mr. Brown, Mr. Blue, Mr. Pink and so on (see Chapter 3).

Strange that throughout the history of dress immense significance has been attributed to a colour which is really a non-colour, as theories and treatises on colour have demonstrated. Goethe and Wittgenstein, for example, have both argued (albeit from different standpoints) that the perception of colour is actually subjective, a modelling activity of the human consciousness, a linguistic game. Black is the obliteration of colour, since it absorbs the whole chromatic range, as opposed to white, which is a synthesis of the primary colours, and the condition for their physical existence and our perception of them. Yet black acts as a clear sign in film and theatrical costume (where every item of clothing is a *total sign*) and always has a precise signification. Linguistically, too, the word 'black' is enriched with further meanings, expressed by terms such as 'dark' and 'noir' that connote not only a chromatic tonality, but also a literary or musical genre, or an atmosphere.

In the film *Men in Black* the prerogative of black clothes to obliterate every recognizable sign on a person is described in Zed's brief to his colleagues, the MiB who control the movements of aliens on our planet:

Zed: You'll dress only in attire specially sanctioned by MiB special services. You'll conform to the identity we give you, eat where we tell you, live where we tell you. From now on you'll have no identifying marks of any kind. You'll not stand out in any way. Your entire image is crafted to leave no lasting memory with anyone you encounter. You're a rumour, recognizable only as *deja vu* and dismissed just as quickly. You don't exist; you were never even born. Anonymity is your name. Silence your native tongue. You're no longer part of the System. You're above the System. Over it. Beyond it. We're "them." We're "they". We are the Men in Black.

In the Italian comic book series *Martin Mystère* by Alfredo Castelli, there is a powerful and invincible secret sect, like MiB, that is the swore enemy of the archaeologist-detective Martin. They too are called 'men in black', because when performing their destructive deeds they wear black suits and ties and dark glasses. Their task is to preserve the secret society from anything that could upset received meaning, from proof of the existence of UFOs, to archaeological and scientific discoveries (the existence of Atlantis, for example). In other words, anything that does not coincide with the official line.

In the above instances, the man's black suit makes explicit an obliteration of meaning, a kind of physical absorption of all light rays that transforms the body dressed in black into a transparent, or invisible, entity and, like camouflage, gives it an absolute anonymity in the crowd, whether the body be that of a bluesman, a criminal or a secret agent. Black for film or theatrical costumes becomes a distinguishing feature and makes a character metonymic with respect to his clothes.

Thus conceived, the black suit is also a travesty of the black dinner jacket worn on formal occasions, the sole function of which is to make the male body completely insignificant as a physical, sensual entity – a prerogative entrusted exclusively to the female body on such occasions, draped in a long, elegant evening gown. The dinner jacket: black, standardized, always the same (summarily speaking). The evening gown: flowing, excessive, revealing, seductive, especially if it is black; the garment of a showpiece body accompanying the more serious patriarch.

Fashion communicates and is reproduced through intertextual strategies that involve different social discourses. The above examples point to the existence of a synergy between fashion as a form of mass communication and other discourses – such as those belonging to the imagery in films and comic books – that circulate tastes and produce styles.

The socio-semiotic definition of style refers to a system of intentional signs with distinctive features that are discontinuous with regard to a presumed 'naturalness'. In his essay 'Style and its Image', Barthes speaks of stylistic features as 'transformations' (1984: 133; see Chapter 3). Not an identity category,[2] therefore, the word 'style' recalls a sort of 'bending' of tastes, whether individual or collective, as well as a logic of otherness, or excess, with regard to a norm.

Black clothes indicate a style in this sense: a system that reformulates and transforms citations and archetypes, that shows how a garment can allude to a whole range of cultural texts and discourses. Gothic, for example, a style (of dress and music) in vogue in the 1980s, was an explicit reference to a literary genre (a genre also exploited by the Hammer House of Horror, the famous British film company). The black, vampire-like garments worn by young Goths at Bauhaus and Sisters of Mercy concerts contrasted with the pallor of their skins, 'incised' with black on lips and eyes. In youth fashion today there is a vogue for black T-shirts with designs that allude to a comic book 'cult of mystery' or refer to heavy metal rock bands. The 1990s male vogue for black shirts, worn without a tie under black jackets, was a reaction against (and parody of) the yuppie's blue blazer of the 1980s. More recently, it has become a knowing and sophisticated citation of appearance styles on the British music scene in the 1950s and 1960s, somewhere between Beatniks and Mods.

Institutional fashion collects and reformulates many of the signs present in different social discourses. With regard to black, there are a few fashion designers who are particularly enamoured of this colour: Yamamoto with his 'essential black', Versace with his 'black image' and Dolce & Gabbana with their 'Mediterranean black' are three such examples.

Yamamoto's case is a special one, since his choice of black is motivated by his search for the essence of a garment, be it for men or women. Yamamoto's clothes are 'pure form' (see Chapter 11); the choice of black for his garments exhibits the body essentially as a silhouette, a form which Barthes defines as 'symbol and sign, fetish and message' (1982: 114).

Versace loved to use black in his fashion creations. His 'little black dress' (1994) is perhaps one of his most memorable garments: a long camisole-dress with a plunging neckline, held together at the waist and shoulders by gilded safety-pins.[3] This garment provocatively inverts the bourgeois role of the classic 'little black dress' as a sign of perennial *bon ton* that every lesson on style advises a woman to keep in her wardrobe. As Richard Martin says, Versace's aim was to shock the middle classes through an ironic and sophisticated use of strategies that play with the role of the media image, somewhere between vulgarity and fetishism, but reformulated in his unmistakable style:

Versace chose as his heroic female model the prostitute or streetwalker, but her transfiguration was into art and media, just as her transmogrification in the 1880s and 1890s under the aegis of Henri de Toulouse-Lautrec was about bringing the vernacular custom of the street into the couture-standard of the art. (Martin 1998)

Dolce & Gabbana's black outfits propose typically Italian, more specifically Mediterranean, imagery.[4] Black for their women's clothes is soft and sensual, for their men's, simple and severe, almost always accompanied by loose, long-sleeved white shirts. Citations from cinema are often explicit in their collections: Italian Neorealism, black and white footage, women who remind us of Anna Magnani in the unforgettable scene of her chasing the Fascist wagon in *Roma città aperta.*

Black is the colour *par excellence* of fetishist clothing (see Steele 1997), clothing that parades, or exhibits, the status of fashion objects and the fashion system in social imagery. Fetishes are inanimate objects, *things*, invested with a power and fascination 'stolen', as it were, from individual sensibility. According to Ugo Volli, the contemporary fascination with fetishes is a kind of metaphor representing the relation between the social subject and consumer objects, a metaphor that concerns, more broadly, the present condition of the consumption of signs, images and bodies (Volli 1997: 102).[5]

For Walter Benjamin, fashion is a celebration of fetishism: on the one hand, it transforms the human body, especially the female body, into the sum of its parts, each of which is considered a cult object in itself; on the other, it is the form in which merchandise, the inorganic object, reveals an unexpected fascination (see Chapter 5).

Many items of fetishist clothing – from silk lingerie to high-heeled shoes, all naturally inspired by the female body – are black. This colour, or non-colour, 'marks' the body with strips of leather, lace and fabrics like silk, satin and velvet. Black thus 'dresses' the female body, incises its skin.

What socio-semiotic explanation can we give to the diffusion of fetishist tastes in fashion, present not just in Versace's collections, but also in more widespread and everyday fashion signs? Perhaps one linked to the fact that, in this way, fashion exhibits its own laws in a strange admixture of erotic games on the body (see Chapter 5). The prerogative of fashion is to mediate between taste and received meaning, a mediation that operates through a special relation between the sign and the senses. Fetishist black in fashion discourse thus has a specific function. Black absorbs the light, obliterates all other colours, evokes darkness and night as zones in which the unforeseen, the unexpected and the unheard become the norm. And so this 'degree zero' of colour becomes a 'black hole' that swallows all the senses and regurgitates them in transfigured forms.

If we were to characterize the contemporary fetishist attitude in terms of gender we would undoubtedly say that it is a male attitude, since it evokes man's socio-cultural possession of the female body and its related imagery. Some scholars, however, have spoken of a female fetishist attitude linked to forms of desire and to imagery elaborated without the mediation of the phallus.[6] Nevertheless, in the social discourse of fashion, it is difficult to establish a clear gender divide. While it is true that such discourse follows the dominant cultural order and appeals to established socio-sexual hierarchies, it is also true that both clothing *bricolage* and, more generally, fashion as an *eccentric* system are situated on the outer limits of this order. And so fetishism can be seen, not as a visual and erotic stereotype, but as a perverse, dissonant and imperfect possibility that, like a black cosmic hole, swallows and reformulates *ex novo* every sign belonging to an established order.

'Wearing black' is an expression with a dual significance: in everyday speech, apart from indicating the act of wearing something black, it can also refer to 'black' as a linguistic term invested with physical and cultural significance (as in 'black' fashion). The 'black' in question is the subject belonging to a 'non-white' human group, whose racial identity is the product of a hegemonic, colonial discourse devoid of any biological or scientific basis. The construction of 'black' as an object of discourse is associated with the social practices of exploitation, violence and segregation that dominant cultural and racial groups have inflicted over the course of history on non-dominant groups.

In the stereotyped images that are part of fashion and mass culture, that of the 'black body' is particularly important. I refer here to the body of the 'black' top model constructed in the hegemonic discourse of 'white' fashion as an artificial body that impersonates an obsessive and animal-like 'naturalness'. Think of Grace Jone's body, whose 'perverse fascination' is associated with feline and masculine images; or of Naomi Campbell's, unnatural to the point of the total cancellation of a salient feature of black identity: her curly hair, which she wears fanatically straight.

bell hooks (1990) maintains that in African-American culture, dress (like music) has always played an important role in forms of self-representation and has always had a political function, especially amongst women, who use style to express resistance or, conversely, conformity. hooks particularly criticizes the exploitation of the image of the 'black beauty' through media figures such as Tina Turner, Iman and Naomi Campbell.

Nevertheless, this is an ambivalent process, since the values at stake in the construction of aesthetic commonplaces are not merely prescriptive and objectifying. For example, the black models, pop stars and athletes idealized by young whites have made it possible to construct cultural spaces for an interaction between bodies that excludes common stereotypes of the black physique and sexuality. This has come about especially through independent modes in the representation and communication of images of black culture; jazz and blues music, for example, and more recently cinema and fashion, to the point of creating actual genres, 'black movies' and 'black fashion'.

In jazz the relation between the garment and music is particularly significant, since jazz represents much more than just a musical genre; it is a veritable universe in which appearance style *counts*. In the 1930s the Zoot style included long, wide jackets, broad-brimmed hats and garish colours – all elements based on hyperbolic exaggeration.[7] In the 1950s, on the other hand, the hipster style, created by musicians like Thelonius Monk, Charlie Parker and Dizzy Gillespie, was more sober and essential. The clothing of female jazz singers, like Billie Holiday, alluded to dress styles typical of the Deep South: soft fabrics, sensual models and floral designs.

Music has always acted as a bridge between black appearance styles and their wider social reception and circulation, even in hybrid forms (see Gilroy 1992). Along with jazz, reggae has played an important role in this, inspired by Rastafarian culture and its icon Bob Marley, with his long, braided locks and parti-coloured clothes. Today hip-hop, its roots in North American black urban communities, proposes open and irreverent forms in a 'street-and-sports' style. Just as everyone can make hip-hop and rap music, so everyone can play basketball, climb walls or bungie jump. Amateur sports imagery, especially that of extreme sports, has invaded the world of fashion with trainers, baggy tracksuits and hooded sweatshirts in the style of black rappers. Black *haute couture* fashion, on the other hand, was successfully launched in the 1990s by African and African-American designers.[8]

The colour black can be an unusual, unheard note; it can be the search for an essence, or it can be citation and contrast. In other words, it is something that produces a particular kind of aesthetic pleasure (not necessarily linked to beauty) that turns the body into a place of passage and transformation (see Chapter 11).

Notes

1. As if to say, you can and can't judge a book by its cover; what's important is that its status is clearly visible.

2. As in the more common, accepted sense of the term.

3. It was worn by Liz Hurley at the opening night of *Four Weddings and a Funeral*.

4. The Mediterranean is the archetypical backdrop for these two Sicilian designers.

5. For the various interpretations of the term 'fetishism', see Chapter 5. In Freudian psychoanalysis the fetish is a substitute for the phallus, the meaning and value of which is removed, and comes to be represented by a single object, perhaps a garment or a certain part of the body.

6. See T. de Laurentis 1997, in which the writer links female fetishism to lesbianism.

7. The most famous exponent of this style was Cab Calloway.

8. The doyen of African fashion is Lola Faturoti. Other names include: Alpha Sidibé, whose name means elephant; Alphadi, who dresses the Senegalese musician Youssou n'Dour; Oumou Sy, a nomad designer who mixes popular styles with technological materials; and Pathé O, who designs Nelson Mandela's shirts. African-American designers, on the other hand, include CD Greene, whose collections are inspired by 1940s and 1950s female jazz singers, Byron Lars, with his 'funky' collection, and Kevin Smith, with his balloon skirts and silk and satin fabrics.

Mass Fashion: The Role of Fashion in Music

Introducing the volume of essays by various authors, *L'aria si fa tesa*, the Italian philosopher, Mario Perniola, recalls the title of a song by the American pop group Primus, 'The Air Is Getting Slippery', as both illustrative and symptomatic of our contemporary state of 'feeling', which, as represented in music, the arts and the mass media, is tense, slippery, ambiguous and unstable. 'The antennae of collective feeling,' writes the author, 'record the advent of forms of unknown experience and present known experience under the guise of something confused and unrecognizable' (Perniola 1994b: 5). Some languages – fashion and music, for example, but also cinema, design and the figurative arts – manage better than others to take on board this tension, this adventure of the senses, which today dictates the fate of social living in an age in which great narratives, especially political narratives, seem to be over and done with. Through modes of dress and music (listened to, danced and performed) the younger generations take on bodily forms of feeling and constructing an identity well before such modes crystallize into ideologies or great social projects. And this is certainly not a novelty of the last decade, nor even less of the postmodern age. The novelty lies, perhaps, in the fact that today there is a widespread perception and awareness of the plurality of languages, registers and available signs, and also of the need to 'listen' to sense experience. Vittorio Castelnuovo summarizes this need by using an expression dear to jazz and rock jargon, of being 'hip on something' (1994: 52).

Fashion and music are two intimately connected forms of worldliness, two social practices that go hand in hand, sustaining one another in the medium of mass communication and drawing on a common sensibility which translates into taste. The first aspect is immediately recognizable in the careful choice of clothes, hairstyles, settings and gestures that accompanies every public perform, video clip or record cover in the music business. Yet the second aspect is surely the more interesting (and is, in any case, the presupposition for the first): how can taste be generated and conveyed through musical experience as both more worldly and at the same time non-conformist? In fashion and music how is the relation between taste and style established? How is one sensibility grafted onto another?

Just as with jazz, with rock one can speak of a genre 'beyond genre' and also beyond music: a universe of choices, values, lifestyles and trends; an imagery open to continuous affiliations, both in a popular context and in one of exploration and experimentation. Castelnuovo speaks of the idea of 'bewildered beauty' to which creativity in rock music is indissolubly linked, and he also refers to a 'frenzy to attain imperfection' (1994: 49). From a semiotic point of view, Greimas sees the concept of imperfection as the unexpected, that which doesn't necessarily lead to pleasure, nor even less to harmony; that which, in causing a rupture with the everyday, transforms and reshapes its subject (see Marrone 1995).

Imperfection in this case concerns that which doesn't stay in place, according to the inverted, disconcerting law expressed by David Bowie, 'If a thing works, throw it away' (Castelnuovo 1994: 49), or Vivien Westwood's 'If the cap doesn't fit, wear it' (Hebdige 1979: 107). This logic of imperfection has governed the different generations of rock music and dress taste, as a kind of cultural *koine* of 'mutiny', each successive generation consciously living anew the state of perceptual and sensory doubt and displacement of the previous generation. And if we want to trace a time graph, this would start with the origins of rock, as a hymn of rebellion, and of political, cultural and aesthetic subversion; next, the destructive affiliation of Punk, a trend which sought to demonstrate the death of the concept of subculture and the anthropological-semiotic mutation of the idea of style; and finally, today's hip-hop, on the cutting edge, open to listening and reproducing the various languages (musical and verbal) of the world, the street and technology through a constant use of sampling and mixing.

Today urban identity is a matter of image, of identity in the midst of the crowd. Yet it is by no means a postmodern problem. At the turn of the century Edgar Allen Poe had already anticipated these themes in his short story 'The Man of the Crowd' (see Chapter 3). The 'world' that populates the modern metropolis is the 'crowd', a 'veil' that hides the mob, a simulacrum of individuals, yet within which everyone displays unmistakable features, as in Poe's short story. In the metropolis the whole worldly dimension of fashion, in its more unusual and unconventional forms, linked to the transitory nature of urban life and to the new speed of communication, is made explicit. From the sense of belonging – the new tribes represented by subcultures and street styles (see Polhemus 1994) – to the creativity of the hieroglyphics and graffiti that 'deface' buildings and subways (see Chambers 1985).

The concept of the clothed body as a grotesque body (see Chapter 3) is the focal point for an inverted and disconcerting aesthetic search for imperfection, expressed through a polyphony of bodies. We find an example of such polyphony in a video from the 1980s that became the emblem of an age and constituted a watershed in the history of this kind of dissemination of music and fashion: 'Thriller' – with a still dark-skinned Michael Jackson and directed by John Landis – where bodies are horribly ugly and deformed. In a carnivalesque inversion of 'modern' and 'primitive', ugly and beautiful, funny and frightening, the screams and the dance generate a kind of fashion that is, above all, confusion and inversion of sense, the call of the street at night as a place where the haphazard is transformed into excess.

Fashion and music are forms of feeling and living in the world, they are languages that construct spaces and identities. In our age of electronic syn thesis and other technical simulacra in the creation, reproduction and execution of the musical score (*sic:* text), fashion and music are measured against the reality of these new media and themselves become new media. Not just in the more strictly technical sense in which musical production, stylistic creation, photography, etc. happen, but above all in the sense that both fashion and music have become imbued with social practices introduced by the new media in the production of discourses and identities.

Let's turn to the spaces that in the last decades have constructed image and sound experiences. The rock concert was a place of bodily 'pluripresences', a place of expanding relational and sensory experience, as the historic encounters of the 1960s and 1970s testify. This is still partly true today for the mega-concerts organized by multinational music companies, as well as for the humanitarian or politically inspired music rallies (Live Aid, for instance). Heretical and technological descendants of the early rock concerts and Punk happenings, were the raves of the early 1990s, which were bodily, rather than musical, performances (the latter being really only secondary). These were places where conflict and rebellion, albeit in post-political garb (see Liperi 1988), found their expressive outlet in 'feeling the beat' and performing through signs on the body. These two types of public event, the concert and the rave, celebrate direct presence, bodily experience and physical contiguity. Dancing, pogoing, taking drugs, having sex, the construction of an external style (hair and dress styles, piercing, tattooing) may be conceived of, yet again, in the light of the grotesque. Lack of diversification (the dance), annihilation in the crowd (the pogo), writing on and incising the skin, loss or amplification of sense perception, a mutual swallowing of bodies, like the Tarot image of the Wheel of Fortune, are all experiences in which space and time are a 'present continuous' becoming.

Both like and unlike bodily experiences lived in the flesh, today's digital, computer and mass media cultures propose spaces and forms for the transmission and reproduction of music and dress experiences that no longer concern the typical 'live' concert or the copy of a 'live' performance on record. The use of electronics, which in rock goes back to the 1960s, video, CD or DVD, Internet sites, a TV channel like MTV amassing viewers from all over the world to experience the latest sounds and dress styles, all show how the production and enjoyment of music is 'wired', hooked up to a machine, part of an interface that uses the human body as an adjunct to a wider nervous system, made up of cables, optic fibres, satellites and microchips.

Talens has expressed these notions using Baudrillard's definition of simulacra, and emphasizing the fact that the function of the media is that of producing sense, establishing norms of communicative exchange and creating spectator, or social subject, typologies (see Talens 1994). With simulacra, writes Talens, we are in the presence of a radical change within an epistemological paradigm: representation has been substituted by simulation. The binary relation between a thing and the sign that represents it – for example, between a musical score and the live performance or analogous recording – has been substituted by the synthesized reconstruction of the thing, the serial reproduction of the event, or its direct creation through the impulses and infinitesimal units of digital information.

Yet simulation still has to do with the body, and the *virtual* nature of communication today is not something immaterial consisting only of bytes and not atoms (see Negroponte 1995). It is rather made up of semiotic material that populates social imagery and taste; the stuff of which, for example, the mutant, postmodern icon of pop, the 'material girl' Madonna, is made. Her body is ancillary to her gear and mutates through time to serve an image. She is the new Zelig: fat, thin, blond, brunette, shaped by grotesque pointed breasts in a Gaultier corset, or wrapped in a sweeping black cloak for the video 'Frozen', where the woman is transformed first into a crow and then into a Doberman in a desert scene inspired by *The English Patient* (see Tancredi 1999).

In terms of this type of semiotic material, we may like to consider the construction of simulacra as contemporary myth, which deprives the sign of its direct representational quality and substitutes it with a serial interchangeability, as in the case of Madonna. On the other hand, our present condition leaves room for sensory forms, especially in fashion and music, geared toward excessive modes, even though they can be created and reproduced serially. Three of these modes are particularly interesting: postcolonial identity, 'surfing styles' and revival.

It's interesting to consider how important the element of appearance style is in the construction of a postcolonial identity. A decentred gaze sees the clothed postcolonial body as an open, grotesque body, adorning itself with colours, signs, jewellery and hairstyles of diverse origin. Postcolonial fashion is made up of the 'surreal everyday' that exaggerates, juxtaposes unpredictably, and quotes self-consciously and deliberately from the world.

The expression 'surfing styles' used by Ted Polhemus, together with 'sampling' and 'mixing' taken from DJ jargon, are effective metaphors in contemporary dress culture. They indicate the overthrow of stylistic and subcultural specificity, in a kind of 'surfing' that recalls the eponymous hypertextual and intertexual 'sport' on computer networks (see Polhemus 1996). For example, everyday street styles that recall the 'bastardized' languages of hip-hop and rap in its rhythmic construction of a sort of *brico-lage*.

Today the case of revival is particularly interesting. Fashion and music have always used citations, experiences, influences and suggestions taken from the past. Fashion in the second half of the twentieth century has steadily shortened the rhythms with which one looks to the past. In this continual spiral it has thus constructed forms of feeling which, although effectively focused on the present, review it and retrace it, not so much through 'historical memory' as through a knowing *mélange* of time fragments and quasi-syncopated images, as in a jazz performance.

The wear-and-tear on signs, or their annihilation even, gives as much pleasure as their creation, not only because such wear-and-tear sets up the expectation of new forms, where tension and desire will be generated, but also because 'consuming' something by wearing it, or putting on used, already worn clothes, is in itself a sense experience. Vintage items and used clothes, today well within the sphere of institutionalized fashion, show how this pleasure corresponds to the taste for wearing clothes that let us live and relive, appropriating as our own, the memories and emotions of others. In this case there is an inversion of the traditional mechanisms of fashion: semiotic wear-and-tear becomes more important than physical wear-and-tear and beats out the rhythms of fashion consumption.

Another motif taken from experimental music and reworked by fashion is chiasmus, when the body becomes the vehicle for a tension between 'natural' and 'artificial', between contrasting styles (gym shoes with a ball gown), or between generations (Dr. Martens with a suit). The logic of dress retraces the logic of music present in so-called 'world' music, in rap and in the contemporary *mélange* of musical genres. The opposition, or balance, between two extremes, the unexpected, unheard note, are all elements that produce a special form of aesthetic pleasure, which makes the body a place of passage and transformation. Thus the sensory dimension becomes a political dimension, since perception and communication consist in opposing received meaning, while at the same time they tend to make 'feeling' common property. Certainly, the garment, the accessory, the body *tout court*, transformed into discourse and communication, are often cheated of their own truth, their adherence to things, their essence, and so become, at best, myth, at worst, idle chatter. Fashion, as a system of images, is transmitted through series and stereotypes, filters in which the image has become an imperative sign. The problem is one of understanding to what extent we perceive the body through the 'already seen' and the 'already felt', and to what extent the fashion image, or rather the not merely visual complexity of the fashion system, manages to activate *aesthesis* as transformation and rupture of the preceding order, as continual excess, and aesthetics as social practice. This is surely the meaning of that rupture with the imperative function of images and, more generally, with the merely visual dimension, which is generated by the relation between fashion and music.

12

Time

Barthes writes that fashion substitutes 'for the slow time of wear, a sovereign time free to destroy itself by an act of annual potlach' (1967: xii). The expression 'sovereign time' shows that the time of fashion is not cumulative, chronological or historical, but a 'wasted' time that exceeds the ordered signs of 'useful' consumption.

Senseless destruction is celebrated by fashion. It is everything that goes beyond the waste predicted by the economic laws of value; even though the 'general economy', as Bataille calls it, always takes into account that there is refuse, or waste, to be destroyed every time energy is produced. Bataille writes that only laughter, parody, irrational consumption and sacrifice escape this economy. They are all part of sovereign time, a time which mocks itself, and ridicules accumulation:

> Above all, the general economy shows that excess energy is produced which, by definition, cannot be used. This excess energy can only be wasted without any purpose, and, consequently, it is senseless waste. Such useless, senseless waste is sovereignty (Bataille, 1973: 284).

The speed of the fashion system renders its mechanisms of production and destruction inaccessible. Potlach imitates consumption as caricature, since it plays at raising the stakes, and does not limit itself to an equal exchange. In this way fashion is part of Bataille's 'sacrifice'; that is, 'not only the rite itself, but every representation or narrative in which the destruction (or threat of destruction) of a hero or, more generally, a being, has an important role' (Bataille 1973: 288).

Everything would be part of the general economy if the destruction were 'real', if the experience of death were a direct experience without mediation. The fashion experience, however, plays on spectacle, on the distance offered by images. Fashion exhibits its production mechanisms in its physiognomy: in this 'ostensive' sense, it is text *and* body, text *as* body, a body where every single sign tells a story. So the time of fashion is consumed in a space where it no longer makes sense to separate past and present, synchrony and diachrony. Both directions, towards the past and towards the present, coexist in what Barthes calls (in a linguistic cast of the term 'utopia') 'uchronia', a time which does not exist, but which can be expressed by both verbal and non-verbal signs. Everything that can be said *about* fashion is said *by* fashion: the meta-discourse of fashion shares with the system it discusses paradoxes and ambitions, masks and transgressions.

Perhaps it was an unknowing semiotic sensitivity towards this status of fashion that lead Leopardi, in *Dialogo della moda e della morte*, to personify fashion. In his dialogue, death and fashion are sisters: 'We were both born of Transience' (1827: 23). They are both part of the ephemeral game of appearances, are both used to 'continually renewing the world' (1827: 24). Leopardi writes that while death turns to 'people and blood', fashion turns to 'beards, hair, household goods, and buildings' (1827: 24). The rites of fashion, like the rites of death, always involve an operation on the body, a sacrifice, a profanity, in which fashion plays at 'perforating ears', 'scorching flesh' and 'deforming people', even at 'stopping their breath', and in which the masks of fashion create models, cover the body's cavities, construct empty spaces or protuberances, thereby generating a 'second body' whose interchangeable and reproducible parts exist as a body with infinite possibilities.

Re-collecting the past is a paradox of fashion: sometimes things from the past become imperative signs in the present, and fashion, which continually renews everything, renews itself by drawing sustenance from the old. For Simmel this is maximum thrift, ironic 'eternal return', a parody of cyclical time, which plays between frugality and excess, repetition and waste. As in the enumeration of Pantagruel-like enormities, the obsessive repetitiveness of fashion revival is a parody of accumulation, a mockery of linear time. In the redundancies of revival, history is tastefully and elegantly acted out. So fashion, apart from being what *goes out* of fashion, as Coco Chanel said, is more than ever, in our postmodern age, what *comes back* into fashion.

In the 1990s, for example, the 1970s were a reference point for both high and street fashion, as well as for the representative images which construct beauty codes. Anyone who has looked at the style of the new divas, the top models, who came on the scene in the last fifteen years of the twentieth century, will have noticed how their bodies were constructed with a nod to the clothed bodies in vogue twenty to twenty-five years before. Claudia Schiffer was a symbol of this body montage in an advertisement for Fanta in the summer of 1993, in which she dances with Mickey Mouse and seems half Brigitte Bardot (thanks to the cleavage and striped T-shirt), half Jean Shrimpton (thanks to the trousers and the low slung chain around her hips).

The past returns, but the retro look is never a mechanical copy of the original. The past is decontextualized of its 'historicity' and style is constructed as a *bricolage* of old and new, a superimposition of different seasons and designs. Dressing from the past is an act, a performance, be it obvious or imperceptible. Thus Claudia Schiffer will never be simply an amalgamation of bodies, she will always have some overriding sign which defines her externally as a woman of her time, and not of the past.

The crocheted tops worn over trousers by young women in the 1990s, for example, were a citation of the late 1960s and the 1970s; they recalled Courrèges tops made of metallic materials, which shocked *haute couture* at the time, and the handmade knits worn by young women at sit-ins. The new twist was that, in the 1990s, they were often worn over a leotard, a garment somewhere between 'under' and 'over', in a game of revealing and concealing typical of more recent fashion. It seems strange to see girls who literally put themselves in their mothers' shoes and even consult old family photos to give them clues about how to dress or do their hair. The mothers, for their part, can rediscover a past which is no longer distant, but rather a time which – thanks to a touch, not of magic, but of fashion – can return, albeit with a few more wrinkles the second time around.

It often happens that fashions seen in photographs, films or videos of times gone by, from the most private to the most public, seem so ugly and in such bad taste that we are ready to swear no one would ever have the courage to bring them back. Yet our eyes get used to them again, and fashion rewrites the concept of beauty. Or rather, it rewrites the laws of what its signs allow, of what we choose to wear, which does not always bear any relation to beauty. Take platform shoes, for example, reintroduced from the 1970s (themselves a revisitation of 1940s fashion), but exaggerated to the point of being grotesque, a caricature 'seasoned' with heterogeneous styles from Heavy Metal to New Romantic. We certainly cannot call them beautiful, yet many people like them and even those who would never wear them are used to seeing them and accepting that even bad taste is permissible.

In this backward movement in time, a classic law of fashion, there is something new: an ethical principle one could say. Looking to the past by dressing from the past seems to be less a matter of fashion, in the institutional sense, and more a matter of *style*, that is, of a broader sharing of experience. This does not necessarily mean that someone who wears clothes from the 1970s and 1980s, particularly a young person, can enter into the mental state of those times and relive history, but they can experience, even if only partially, some of the values from those years and compare them to the present.

I have a treasured memory of wearing second-hand clothes. An organza dress made by a famous Viennese tailor bought for 5,000 Lire at the Porta Portese market one Sunday morning in the late 1970s. When I wore that starched, calf-length dress, with a narrow waist, filled out by a petticoat, as they used to wear in the 1950s, patterned with pastel flowers sketched on white and leaving my shoulders bare, I felt like a modern day Grace Kelly. I wore it happily to parties and on evening strolls on those summer nights accompanied by the sounds of the first 'free' radio stations.

Indeed, from the 1960s to the 1970s, we were part of a whole generation that bought second-hand clothes in specialized shops which sprang up everywhere, or in markets like Porta Portese and Portobello Road, where second-hand clothing was mixed with antiques and 'poor' fashion with everyday art. We came home from the second-hand markets with jackets, dresses and coats all from one harvest and smelling of mothballs. After a good clean they lived new stories on new bodies, hiding, yet at the same time showing through small signs, their mysterious past.

Then came the 1980s, the 'designer' 1980s, the decade of the Collections, of euphoria for institutionalized fashion which, even though not accessible to everyone, could at least be copied or faked. Second-hand, the 'low' end of fashion, made way for fakes. The most famous market for this in Italy was the Forcella Market in Naples, whence imitation Lacostes, Levis and Guccis soon spread throughout the country.

In the 1990s second-hand was once again a fashion phenomenon. The neo-consumerism of designer labels and ephemeral clothes, available only to an élite, made way for cult or second-hand 'labelled' dressing. European cities from Florence to London and Paris were once again full of second-hand shops. And not only the big cities: in Italy, for example, one famous temple of second-hand clothing is the *Vintage Palace* in Lugo, a small town in Emilia Romagna. These are places where different generations, different subjects, create on their bodies, and according to their own sense of taste, appearance styles through which they can construct an identity.

Let's follow at random one of these 'subjects'. A girl goes into a shop wearing jeans and a cut-off vest top, her hair cropped short, like Demi Moore in *G.I. Jane*, but she is fresher, more genuine, than any up and coming Hollywood star. She is not a top model, but a pop model, an everyday model, who manages to give meaning to a gesture, a hairstyle, a garment in any modern context. And it is a specific garment the girl is looking for: a pair of pre-1970s jeans with a low waist and wide bottoms, not exactly flares, but something close. Wearing second-hand clothes, putting on part of the past recontextualized in the present, reliving the signs and atmosphere of twenty to twenty-five years ago, feeling they are as much ours as anyone else's, is a widespread vogue of fashion revival, or 'vintage' as it is called.

Undoubtedly, second-hand clothes have always been worn. Apart from the logic of the consumer market and fashion, the Salvation Army, churches, and humanitarian organizations have always collected clothes and accessories to give to the poor. There have always been daily second-hand markets for the buying and selling of wedding dresses, fur coats, quality shoes and baby outfits. It is also normal amongst friends and relatives to hand down children's clothes, since children have a naturally ephemeral wardrobe. The more these phenomena exist, the more the well-being of the middle classes declines and the army of needy people grows.

Today second-hand clothing produces a variety of appearance styles: the 'designer label game' is one of these, as is rediscovering old subcultures by recycling their signs and bringing them up to date in a veritable clothing ecology. Wearing or collecting old clothes never means mechanically repeating the past or aping history; it means, rather, experiencing new feelings and new stories in those everyday coverings we call clothes. It is, moreover, an appearance style in harmony with a new ethic of thrift (see Chapter 3). So wearing second-hand clothes is today even less a matter of fashion, or of an identifiable subcultural style; it is rather an experience happening in many environments and in multiple discourses, where what is at stake is the relation between taste as received meaning and less conventional forms of sense experience.

If Roland Barthes had written his *Mythologies* twenty years later than its actual publication (1957), along with the Tour de France, he might have included the parka, the symbolic uniform of young people inaugurated in 1968. The Frenchman might have had to choose Italy instead of France, though, as his preferred observatory, since this garment was more popular there than elsewhere. He might also have had to deal with the fact that, as he himself wrote in 1971, the decoding of contemporary myth had itself become 'mythical' and had penetrated received meaning.

In those years, however, none of the young people in parkas thought about decoding what they were wearing, since what they wore was intended to be part of an 'anti-fashion' that claimed to wipe out institutionalized habits, including having to explain why one chose to dress in a certain way. If a young person were asked why, out of so many beautiful jackets, they had chosen that horrible green sack, they would instantly reply that it was just something to keep out the cold and that it was cheap.

No choice of style or sense of belonging to a group: these worries were left to sociologists in the 'superstructures', not to those who, in their parkas, had to worry about organizing a demonstration at school or university the next day or handing out leaflets in front of factories at dawn. Students hoped to cancel out their privileges there, close to the proletariat, to those who had been wearing that ugly jacket for decades.

It is important to attribute values to objects (including clothes) that derive from lived experiences, which they have in some way distilled, and not from projections of our prejudices. It is in these projections that myth is created as 'linguistic theft' and in the distorted memory of the 'parka generation', as seen through the eyes of its executors, which include some of its protagonists, the parka has become a myth *in spite of* itself. Yet in its role as an object-symbol of anti-fashion, the parka can claim to be totally non-mythical, to be made of totally different material from myth.

Young people today have learnt to dress with 'know-how', which is not simply looking for a label or a model to copy at all costs, nor is it simply an excessive Americanism on the basis of which young people look for famous labels of jeans or sportswear just to pay homage to a multinational uniform. It can also be the search for a style, for a way of thinking with mind *and* body, of keeping clothes *and* thoughts in the wardrobe. 'Naïve' signs like the parka would have no meaning nowadays. So we should perhaps ask ourselves how something becomes a myth in spite of itself, yet without raising apocalyptic suspicions of novelty, suspicions that recreate the myth with all its anomalies.

Time is a word laden with philosophical meanings and values, even though it is one of the words most often uttered in daily discourse, such as in the stereotyped formula of 'I haven't got time to'. We measure time on ourselves thanks to the watch, an object worn by almost everyone, which has become a prosthesis of our body and has created automatic and rhythmical movements, like lifting our wrist to look at the time. Watch time is an artificial, conventional time created by the instrument itself. Each of us has our own perception of time, depending on our convictions, routines and speculations, though, as St. Augustine said, when it comes to explaining time things get complicated. We can imagine time as an enormous sphere surrounding us, that contains many possible paths, from that of memory, to that of the body's biological rhythms, nature, the seasons and productive cycles. None of these paths, except the last, is measured by the watch, whose prerogative is to divide time according to a social convention, which to us seems completely natural.

Having a watch on our wrist or in our pocket to consult whenever we want to has not always been a human prerogative. Clocks in miniature only made their appearance at the end of the fifteenth century. The fashion spread first through the upper classes and then, fairly quickly, to the new middle classes. The watch gave people a private measure of time, albeit regulated by public convention, a measure that went perfectly with the rise of modern individualism. Instead of depending on the church bells or the cry of the sentinel, time began to depend on the individual, and the watch began to mark the rhythms of daily life and to organize it. The wristwatch appeared at the start of the twentieth century, when the male waistcoat, with a pocket for the hob watch, began to go out of fashion. Women, too, could wear watches on their wrist; having previously worn them as pendants round their necks or set into rings, they could now use the watch as a practical instrument, not just as a piece of jewellery.

There is, however, an inherent aesthetic value to the watch that goes beyond its chronometric function, symptoms of which can be seen, for example, in the initiatory role of the first watch in a child's life, or in the mania for collecting watches. The ingenious invention of the Swatch interprets the peculiar status of the watch in the object system and has contributed to opening up new frontiers within it.

Born simply as the Swiss watch, sold at a low price, but designed in an eccentric and appealing way, often by famous artists, the Swatch became a contemporary myth in little over a decade, a myth in which a sense of the ephemeral and a passion for collecting are paradoxically combined. The Swatch is a disposable object, made of resistant but inexpensive materials; it continually changes colour and design. Yet it contains something both unique and contradictory: it is a serial object that denies being one. If, on the one hand, the Swatch is a consumer object that is changed as easily as one's clothes, and thus has 'secularized', so to speak, the sacred aura around the measurement of time, on the other, its market laws have produced an unusual form of collecting. Any model can be taken off the market without warning and so become very rare and acquire an exorbitant value. The mania for collecting as many as possible is fuelled by its accessible price and titillated by the secret hope that one day the collector could find her/himself the happy owner of an object of immense value, as happened with the Kiki Picasso and Velvet Underground Swatch.

The history of the Swatch seems to bring together the histories of time, fashion and collecting: it is an object that measures not only time, but also style and, while born of the serial reproduction of the market, breaks its rules, thereby gaining a place in the most famous auction houses and exhibitions halls. Every Swatch owner feels not so much potentially rich as similar to an art or antiques collector, whose wealth is symbolic. Tribes of Swatchers queue outside shops and gather at exhibitions and publicity shows; they read a specialized magazine and exchange catalogues with price lists and collector's items, like teenagers with football stickers. The unusual form of collecting introduced by the Swatch, unlike that of collecting antiques, which devitalizes objects by turning them into fetishes, is oriented towards 'live' objects, objects that continue to function and to live materially.

After the invasion of digital numbers the Swatch reintroduced the round face, traditional numbers and hands. Meta-watches have even appeared, which discuss their own function with slogans like 'Don't be too late' and 'You don't live in a nine to five world' dedicated to the anti-yuppie mentality of the 1990s. Swatch also succeeded in breaking the clockwise taboo in a model in which the hands go backwards. The Swatch phenomenon has introduced unusual forms of communication and consumption: having been an instrument of precision or an item of jewellery, the watch has become a cult object in the paradoxical form of a disposable object to keep. In this way it has combined two trends of the last decades: the passion for everyday objects from the recent past, like fridges from the 1950s and 1960s, which are now valued at thousands of pounds, and widespread urban myths about keeping useless things, for example, the belief in the 1960s that collecting tinfoil could help human-itarian projects.

But let's give a bemused thought to those people who don't wear watches, for whom time manages to measure itself without one. Refractory about the individual chronometer, they make us wonder what the world would be like if we returned to a public measurement of time, with church bells or the sentinel's cry, or even further back, with the sun and the stars. This is wishful thinking: today's world would not give us these archaic, idyllic scenes, but a dark universe like that in *Blade Runner*, where an elec-tronic voice tells the time, resounding in small microchips inside our bodies. The thought is terrifying, so perhaps it's better to linger in Swatchmania, enjoying the fact that the watch can still tell stories and act almost as a living body that prevents our bodies from finally succumbing to a totalitarian time.

A watch made by Coinwatch in 1996 called the 'Six Six Edition' was a limited edition of 1,000. On its face was a reproduction of a silver medal with a picture of the earth and a chronometer that counted down to the third millennium day by day. The owners of these watches could thus greet every morning of this countdown with anxiety, nostalgia or optimism, as the rite required. It was to be expected: the millennium countdown was like the last kilometre of a bicycle race.

Waiting for the fateful date, we seemed to be living in a state of continual expectation of what would be, as the big 'universal' deadlines character-izing the 1990s have shown: celebrations for the fifth centenary of Columbus' voyage, universal exhibitions, epic Olympics and finally (or firstly, who knows?) the designation of the year 2000 as a Holy Year. *Waiting*, then, was the passion that characterized the end of the twentieth century, a wait characterized not so much by those feelings of 'a village Saturday' typical of every important eve, as by the daily anticipations of tomorrow, which allow us to live the present as a surrogate of values, actions and fashions until recently considered the exclusive dominion of an indistinct future.

In this sense the contribution of the new media has been very important, with the laptop in first place, given the radical revolution they have introduced in the pace of life, as well as in ways of communicating, thinking and learning 'online'. Alongside this revolution (which Nicholas Negroponte calls 'the transformation of atoms into bytes') there are others, linked to the objects around us.

Modern science fiction imagery, from Jules Verne to Philip Dick, has shown itself to be a fertile inspiration for and anticipation of present reality. This reality has led us, in a very short time, to wear almost exclusively fabrics made of carbon fibre, polyurethane, rubber or plastic, which are no longer sewn but soldered, cut by laser, enriched with liquid crystals or crystals sensitive to thermofusion, so that they 'mutate' according to light and temperature; all very *Blade Runner*.

There was no need to wait for 2000, materials like these already inhabited our wardrobes and some of them were even 'ancient', if we consider lycra, microfibre, pile and titanium of which stockings, underwear, weatherproof jackets, boots, bags and glasses are all made. The diffusion is even greater than we think: the future is already here. Rollerblades, objects of the new metropolitan *flâneurs*, are made of super-resistant glass and nylon, while among women's stockings there is now *teint soleil*, a garment without seams and with a special polyurethane thread which makes it invisible and heat resistant. In the world of fashion design companies have launched 'cyborg' fabrics and set up projects for the recovery of industrial 'archaeological' finds. Not the stuff of dreams, but of the reality in which we are living.

In the 1960s avant-garde designers like Courrèges and Paco Rabanne had already designed space tracksuits and titanium mini-dresses, but they remained artistic experiments, a fashion destined to be the fashion of the future. Today, however, what we call the 'future', or rather its public representation, does not need to be anticipated because it has already slipped into our daily lives, where it coexists peacefully with totally opposite trends, such as the rehabilitation of natural fibres – cotton, wool and silk – which none of us had ever really stopped wearing, but which fashion discourse has recently exalted as an absolute novelty because they are 'ecological'.

The countdown was not really very useful then, since '2000' had already said all there was to say. So it might be better to count ahead, with no limits, taking inspiration from Stanley Kubrick's film *2001* whose title underlines, in the addition of one unit to the round figure, that tomorrow is not a deadline, but an open window, an uneven number that says not 'year 0' but 'year 1'.

Nowadays there are many objects which keep track of time and each of them, from watches to diaries to calendars, have an important role in our everyday perceptions, beliefs and routines, not just as functional objects for measuring days and hours, but as micro-narratives that express our relation to Chronos. Every new year, whether consciously or not, we rethink or confirm these self-expressions, and this is translated into our choice of a calendar for home, work, or for our friends.

With the huge choice on offer, from the most serious to the most frivolous, the glossiest, the most daring and the most desired on the walls of western men is the Pirelli calendar. Having been on the scene for around forty years, the multinational tyre (and more recently cable) manufacturers' annual publication represents 'keeping time' in a unique way, since, as everyone knows, on its pages are photographs of the most beautiful women in the world. A unique and ingenious coincidence: time and the body come together, every month has the name of a woman, the image of whose body has the task of pervading the days as they pass.

Much more than with voyeurism, here we are in direct contact with distant tales, reverberating in social imagery, such as the myth of eternal youth that the models' perpetually fresh skin seems to allude to, in contrast to the arrows of time that move inexorably forward. Or, for the more apocalyptic, the photographs could be a postmodern, secularized version of images of death dressed as a beautiful, seductive woman that once filled iconography, especially in the baroque period, as a kind of *memento mori*. Undoubtedly, proud owners of the Pirelli calendar do not give much thought to this 'learned' origin of their cult object. Yet in every human passion, there are always vestiges of other passions, in virtue of a generalized intertextuality of culture, and every object, even the most standardized and vulgar, is a sign that recalls other signs and has manifold paths of interpretation.

The Pirelli calendar is an object that has always wavered, in its choice of consumer, between collectors and the general public. Indeed, it began life as an object for a select few, the company's clients, and so was already a potential collector's item. If we go over its history we even find 'legends', like the story of its origins in 1964 in the lively milieu of Swinging London. Robert Freeman, who shot the photographs for the first calendar, was an important protagonist on this scene (he was the Beatles' photographer and a member of a famous group of East End photographers). In these first photographs the models' presence is almost casual, in that the photographs mainly depict the tyres and vehicles on which they are mounted. They are photographs with a precise denotative function, that of describing the goods produced by Pirelli.

In the following years this function linked to the product became less important, compared to the seductive models and the settings. Those of the 1969 calendar were famous, shot on Californian beaches with non-professional models and a total surfing feel. For the 1972 edition Sarah Moon, the first female photographer to work on the calendar, created one with collectors in mind, with the pages of each month separated by photographs. This was the start of a black market trade in the pictures, which were framed and resold for hundreds of pounds each.

Collecting and fetishism are always closely related, as they were with the Pirelli calendar even after the company decided not to publish it any more following the petrol crisis in 1974. In the absence of the real thing the discourses surrounding it proliferated and its luxury value increased. Amongst the more famous discourses was the 'biography' of the calendar written by the actor David Niven in 1975; amongst the luxury locations, Christie's, where ten copies were auctioned for charity in the same year.

The calendar reappeared ten years later and its photographs were a test bed for experimental techniques where the discourses of photography and fashion intersected. This was the 1980s, when fashion completed its transformation into a self-sufficient and authoritative means of mass communication. Pirelli opened its doors to the top models who were most seen on the catwalks of the time, Anna Anderson and Imam, and who were portrayed in the 1985 calendar wearing clothes printed with an image of the P6 tyre. And in 1986 it was down to students at the Royal College of Art to paint women wearing only P6 tyres, that inspired Bert Stein's photographs for the calendar.

The P6 was once again an important part of the 'body to body' with the models in the 1989 edition, which was produced by Joyce Tenneson, the calendar's second female photographer. The relation between fashion and the calendar became even closer, as shown by the thirtieth anniversary edition, published in 1994 and created by Herb Ritts, with photographs of the world's most famous models, and the 1997 edition, dedicated to 'women of the world' by its creator Richard Avalon.

The latter edition seemed to illustrate particularly well how this little contemporary myth, the Pirelli calendar, manages to express tastes and values which correspond to the received meaning of female beauty, albeit in an ambivalent way. Indeed, the 'women of the world' were famous models of different geographical origin, in homage to a political correctness which photography and fashion had by then espoused. From the Brazilian Melanie Britti, who adorns the cover, to the Chinese Ling, the Italian Monica Bellucci, the American Brandi and the Somalian Waris, all faces, bodies, and presumed 'races' and 'ethic backgrounds' are represented. All sizes, too, since well-endowed fitness and white teeth enthusiasts are not the only ones to be seen on its pages, but also exponents of other worlds, where food, fitness and wealth are not taken for granted.

Images of men next to the customary beautiful women were introduced for the first time in 1998. The interesting thing about this system of 'equal opportunities' is that while the women depicted continued to represent symbols of beauty, the men were chosen on the basis of their social role – writers, actors, wealthy business men, and so on – regardless of aesthetic ideals. The stereotype that the calendar continues to advocate is thus the age-old separation of body and mind, sexuality and productivity, pairs in which the first category is associated with the woman and the second with the man. True, when transferred to the glossy pages of the Pirelli calendar, these dichotomies seem to be a mere semblance of reality; the real women and men 'of the world' are perhaps elsewhere.

13

Fashion Intertexts

The great Italian outfitters specializing in priests' cassocks are unanimous: until a few years ago about 70 per cent of the clergy preferred wearing a dog collar, jacket and trousers, but recently there has been a move in the opposite direction and now the younger generations tend to prefer the 'old-fashioned' cassock and no longer desire, as in the 1970s, to look like the man-in-the-street.

There is a saying in Italian 'l'abito non fa il monaco' meaning 'wearing a habit doesn't necessarily make you a monk', a somewhat trite proverb, which apart from its metaphorical implications, might make us wonder whether there is indeed a history of ecclesiastical dress comparable to that of secular dress, and linked in some way to the laws of fashion. The answer is yes, since not only is it possible to record changes in ecclesiastical dress over the centuries, but it is also possible to attribute a social significance to these changes.

It is well known that ecclesiastical vestments take on a ritual significance during the celebration of Mass, and this function is verifiable in sacred representations in all religions, while the significance of those items which are typical of the upper echelons of the Church – such as the mantle, tiara, slipper and mitre – is linked to a specific office. Indeed, the Schism of 1159 began on account of the *immantatio*, the act of putting on the papal mantle: Federico Barbarossa's candidate actually snatched the holy mantle from Alexander III during the latter's investiture and proclaimed himself Pope Victor IV.

The dual nature, at once humble and aristocratic, of the Roman Catholic Church has always been reflected in ecclesiastical dress codes, oscillating between the pomp and extravagance of the papal courts and the simplicity of the mendicant orders.[1] In *Vite dei romani pontefici*, Anastasio quotes a description (dated AD 817) of one of Pope Paschal I's robes, decorated with gold and precious gems, and another robe made entirely of gold cloth. In the eleventh century Pier Damiani inveighed against prelates wearing costly furs, such as sable and ermine, instead of the more modest sheepskin, and in 1127 the Council of London forbade all nuns (including abbesses) from wearing any fur except cat!

The fact that the dog collar is losing ground is undoubtedly a sign of the times, a conservative backlash in the Catholic world sanctioned by 'Woytilanism'. And yet the Vatican doesn't disdain promoting the most kitsch forms of mass communication, such as the young American 'papists' welcoming John Paul II with all kinds of pious trinkets and gadgets (including fake tiaras), like children in Disneyland wearing Mickey Mouse hats. The aristocratic times of Pius XII[2] are long gone, as too are the times of Don Milani and his anti-conformist *Lettera a una professoressa* (1967), a famous essay on the need to abolish class distinctions within the educational system.

While priests are returning to the rigours of the cassock, nuns seem quite stable in their choice of a more secular habit. Whatever happened to the sister in the white wing-tipped coronet? Toscani used it a few years ago in his notorious photo of a nun kissing a priest (who was wearing a traditional cassock), but it was only a whiff of déjàvu. Today nuns have other things on their mind, from the priesthood for women to sexual distinctions in theology.

For her part, the Madonna, that supreme model of femininity, is keeping up with the times, trying to look as postmodern as possible, just as she did in one of her presumed apparitions in eastern Slovenia, where she manifested herself wearing a gold dress and crown à la Barbie, without veil or rosary. The blood-tears of many statues of the Madonna may be taken as an organic metaphor for a bodily covering that recounts her sad stories as conceived in the collective imagination. Interesting that while Madonnas in the West produce liquids, whether tears or blood, in the East there have been cases reported of sacred statutes actually absorbing liquids!

Certainly, more ink has been consumed on the Devil's apparel than on God's *look*. Perhaps rightly so, since dress always contains a diabolical rhetoric.

A few years ago in Southern Italy a very strange bank robbery took place: in order to hide his face the robber covered it, not with a mask, but with a pair of boxer shorts! The episode both mocked and evoked the imagery we usually associate with a criminal's clothing. An Italian cartoon hero, Diabolik, is emblematic of this kind of imagery: with a black stocking over his head, he is transformed from a 'normal' person into a dangerous, yet fascinating, criminal. The black stocking acts as a kind of initiation robe, turning him into a recognizable type. Clothes and style (perhaps expressed through a minor detail) thus become commonplaces through which we can imagine the figure of the criminal.

These commonplaces draw on daily news bulletins, as in the case of the bank robber with boxer shorts (providing us with a bizarre inventory of the criminal's wardrobe), as well as on representations invented by mass communication, literature and cinema. While cartoons offer us Diabolik's stocking-mask and Disney's Basset Band in numbered red T-shirts, the Western depicts the villain in a shabby duster, with a bandana round his neck ready to hide his face when he robs the next stagecoach or bank. In *Reservoir Dogs*, Tarantino imagines metropolitan crooks dressed like the Blues Brothers (see Chapter 10); Bigelow in *Point Break* has her bank robbers wear masks of recent United States presidents; and in Kubrick's *A Clockwork Orange* before committing a crime, the thugs, who all wear white, perform an elaborate dress and makeup ritual on themselves.

As cinema reveals, crime can be seen as a grotesque and provocative performance, a public exhibition that requires the right clothes, whether for practical[3] or spectacular reasons. Yet body signs also speak a secret language of recognition within criminal groups themselves: for example, the expensive, flashy ring worn by the Mafia boss on his little finger.

Rather than flaunting its distinctive features, however, the criminal's body often seeks absolute anonymity. Terrorists, for instance, usually conduct a normal life (even in terms of their external body signs, such as clothes and hairstyle) while they are planning and perpetrating their crimes.[4]

Actually the notion of crime is always relative to a social definition of what is legal or illegal. And this is true both for what we define as crime *tout court* and for the criminal *sign*: until recently western societies considered the tattoo, for example, a mark of deviancy, whereas it is now a respectable and highly desirable fashion sign. The prostitute's outfit, too, now takes on high-profile, aristocratic connotations in the right contexts: night clubs and television shows (see Chapter 5) which allow for the diffusion of otherwise lamentable tastes.

In the light of such rich and complex imagery, we might ask ourselves: how and why we are led to believe that a person is dangerous because of the way s/he looks (that totality of expressive signs, including dress and appearance style, based on individual choice)? Isn't there a risk of social stereotyping in our evaluations, springing from a mechanism of self-defence? Notwithstanding stereotypes, the truly dangerous criminal is the unpredictable one, obsessively, pathologically, even diabolically overturning his/her social role or function: the policeman's uniform that hides the blade of a serial killer; the magistrate's gown, a wad of banknotes; the priest's cassock, the squalid body of a paedophile. A rich inventory of images tapped by literature and cinema alike, but also part of the non-fiction of daily life, as we sadly learn from the news every day. So perhaps the old adage that 'wearing a habit doesn't necessarily make you a monk' (or a criminal either, for that matter) still has some meaning in our everyday life.

Recently an 'anti-snatch' shoe was launched as one of the most innovative accessories in contemporary fashion. Its miraculous function is that of containing a hidden compartment for documents, credit cards and cash. Actually this invention is based on well-known habits for those who live in big cities, where you don't have to keep up with the latest trends to know that it's important to protect your belonging from the very real risk of bag-snatchers and muggers. Hiding money and valuables in shoes or socks is, in any case, a consolidated practice, one of the age-old commonplaces of travel imagery.

Indeed, travel has always been an occasion for inventing ways to safeguard one's belongings. Hidden pockets in clothing and underwear, secret drawers in suitcases and trunks, and shoes with a hollow heel have all served this purpose with varying degrees of success. Today fashion has learnt this lesson: for instance, several companies produce a particular type of unisex traveller's jacket fully kitted out with pockets and hidden recesses of every shape and size for maps, tickets, valuables and so on.

Yet whoever lives in a big city knows that even when crossing the street in front of your house you risk getting mugged, and so it's important to take precautions. So the idea of the anti-snatch shoe may be added to a whole variety of personal techniques for hiding what we don't want others to grab. In terms of clothing imagery, these techniques are mechanisms for 'incorporating' our belongings, so to speak, practically inside ourselves, mechanisms which the fashion industry has taken up in various expedients.[5]

Now that cash has been largely replaced by 'virtual money' (i.e. cashpoint and credit cards) it's easier to protect oneself from theft, at least symbolically, although there is still the risk of cloning. So perhaps it's better to go out with nothing on at all that can expose us to unsolicited adventures. Such a conclusion, now widely held, has had a direct influence on both male and female clothing practices. Women's handbags, for example, have seen the almost total disappearance (for ecological reasons too) of the classic bag with short handles in crocodile or snake-skin (so popular in the 1950s and 1960s), which has now become a museum piece. Shoulder-bags and rucksacks are widely used by both sexes today, while the briefcase (still a conspicuous container of valuables) has various anti-theft and 'body-clinging' devices. Another new object (invented by fashion houses in the 1990s) is the anatomical shoulder-bag, with a long strap, that follows the body's contours.

The anti-theft trend has influenced jewellery too: very few women walk around today wearing the family heirlooms. After having long been relegated to 'the poor', costume and silver jewellery, whether costly or bought from street-vendors, is now very popular, and the fashion for African, Asian and South American jewellery represents a unique blend of stylistic influences: folk costume, on the one hand, and the urban anti-theft fashion for non-precious jewels, on the other.

Thus different signifying systems (evaluative and emotional) meet on our bodies and construct our appearance styles. Fear of theft is one of these, and yet there is something that cannot be 'stolen' from us: our bodies, unless we are kidnapped for ransom, in which case the body represents, not itself, but money.[5]

The history of the relation between fashion and sport is the history of a two-way relation: on the one hand, there is the direct intervention of the fashion designer in the world of sport, while on the other, there is the equally important influence of sport on fashion.

Pioneer of the alliance between designers and sports is the Italian Olympic ski champion, Emilio Pucci, who became famous after the war for a photo session in Harper's Bazaar that depicted him on the slopes of Mount Zermatt wearing some of his own creations. Pucci is also famous for redesigning the uniform of the Italian football team, *La Fiorentina*, with its emblematic lily. Valentino and Ferragamo, for their part, designed the entire wardrobe of the Italian Olympic teams at Los Angeles and Seoul. And when Giorgio Armani's home-town football team, *Il Piacenza*, was promoted to the First Division in 1993, he designed shirts, socks, tracksuits, suits and ties for the players in that most popular and universal of games.

Moreover, the fashion laws of taste and change are clearly visible in the models and fads in sports gear of every type. We need only look at photos of Jesse Owens at the 1936 Olympics or famous footballers from the 1950s to realize just how much the appearance style of professional sportsmen and women has changed over the last decades, and how much more present are fashion and its norms today in the world of sport. This is due mainly to the fact that sport itself has become a big business, and so even uniforms are sponsored. Every day we see ads on TV (for clothes, shoes, perfumes) peopled by the famous names and faces of sports champions.[6]

The norms of the sports *look* vary according to the type of activity: in tennis and golf, traditionally games for the rich, the aesthetic factor is prominent, while in swimming and skiing, clothes subserve technical performance. Nevertheless, the onlookers' aesthetic admiration is clearly sought here too. As for the body, it is also subject to modification: swimmers shave theirs completely, whole football teams dye their hair platinum blond, cyclists wear little goatee beards. And so the dividing line between competitive and seductive strategies is no longer visible.

Today nothing is left to chance in sports gear, with the curious exception of the athletes from the independent states of the former Soviet Union, who in 1992 were still wearing T-shirts with *CCCP* printed on them, since there wasn't any money to buy new ones. Thus, even in the world of sport, fashion is a symptom of history.

Coco Chanel found inspiration in the world of sport, especially water sports, for her popular sweaters and trousers for women, which she 'stole' from men's wear. It is to her that we owe the twentieth century philosophy of 'sporting fashion', that is, of proposing as everyday, casual wear garments and cuts typical of sporting contexts (sailing, tennis, golf and horse-riding in particular). But lately a new factor has been conditioning the relation between sport and fashion: sports gear is no longer seen as something distinct and separate from more elegant or formal attire. The mania for doing sport at all costs has insinuated itself into every nook and cranny of daily life: so the gym top is worn at work under a cardigan, the sweatshirt left on in the office after the morning jog. Tokens of the illusion of an athletic life, at least in terms of appearance.

In times of peace the open wound in the collective sensibility caused by the violence of war remains as an ever-present memory and as a sign which prompts reflection on the more habitual, frivolous and ephemeral aspects of life. Fashion is commonly considered one of these; indeed, its chief characteristic is that of signalling changes in everyday life. In the relation between war and fashion, however, the idea of death and the consumption of bodies and values is common to both (see Leopardi 1827). And this relation has been well documented: in the twentieth century, fashion witnessed tremendous upheavals during the periods of world war. In women's fashion the First World War marked the passage from long to short skirts and, generally, to more sober, essential models, which was also in keeping with the aesthetics of the artistic avant-garde of the time. World war, impoverishing nations, shattering empires and for the first time mobilizing the masses, left its signs on the clothed body too. The essentiality of forms made possible the enjoyment *en masse* of models once only available to the privileged few. As Laura Piccinini (1991) writes, the army clothed bodies: the trench coat was used by the British in the trenches; the Burberry was the raincoat of the RAF; and the cardigan was used in the Crimean War by the British cavalry under the command of Lord Cardigan.

One could write a whole book on fashion around the time of the Second World War, when the global, mass dimension of both turned them into everyday phenomena. Well-known couturiers designed the troops' uniforms, some of which, like the Waves (reserves of the US Marines), became famous. At the same time, rationing imposed limitations on fashion: in 1941 the British government restricted the use of artificial silk (from which parachutes were made) in the manufacture of women's stockings. It was the *sock shock*: socks came to replace stockings, soon becoming a familiar item that was to remain a distinctive sign of teenage fashion even after the war.

In the early 1940s women's clothing took on a more masculine and military appearance (for example, wide shoulders and short, straight shirts), and hair and nails were worn short too. So women experienced in fashion the moderation that was for men part of wartime routine. On an imaginative level, especially thanks to cinema, the military austerity of the 'soldier's gal' was accompanied by the dream of the winsome Hollywood pin-up, epitomized by Gilda, whose name even baptized US aerial bombs.[12]

Fashion photography and war photography merged: for example, in Cecil Beaton's photo of a model standing in the midst of bombed out rubble (British *Vogue* September 1941). And Second World War garments became clothing classics: the RAF bomber-jacket; Clark's desert boots worn by General Montgomery's troops at El Alamein; and the duffel coat worn by the General himself, incidentally, called in Italian a 'Montgomery' (see Piccinini 1991).

In Italian the word 'moda' (fashion) derives from 'modello' (model) and from the Latin word 'modus', meaning norm, rule, measure. Both root words are linked etymologically to 'moderno' (modern), a concept that springs to mind whenever we speak of fashion. In the twentieth century fashion has oscillated between the two thematic and etymological poles of 'model' and 'modus'. When the former prevails, fashion is conceived as the imagined shape of signs and values only available to an élite, while when the latter prevails, fashion becomes a system of rules and values shared by wider social circles. In the past the prevalence of 'modus' was verified in times of war, while since the 1950s it has become the dominant tendency in peace time too.

Since the Second World War, other wars have influenced fashions and anti-fashions. Vietnam, for example, represented a sort of zeroing of fashion imagery, especially in youth culture, which saw its rules and models as ultra-conformist and ultra-establishment. In the 1960s and 1970s the young people in the West who demonstrated against the war in Vietnam rejected all symbolic forms of power, including fashion, which was seen as a capitalist and pro-imperialist enterprise.

The Gulf War in 1991 was the first mass media war witnessed minute by minute by TV viewers, for whom the social landscape of the Persian Gulf, with all its dramatic human events, became a familiar one, as did the soldiers' uniforms, and the gas masks and helmets worn by soldiers, journalists and children alike. And fashion designers had something to say about this war: some cancelled their January shows (the month of Operation Desert Storm); others, like Benetton, used a war cemetery in one of their advertisements; while others, like Moschino, introduced the peace symbol next to their own label on garments. After its heyday in the 1960s, this symbol came back in vogue in the 1990s, on T-shirts, badges and so on. Wherever and whenever there is a war raging it is present as a potent sign of international pacifism: in Bosnia, Palestine, Afghanistan, Iraq.

When war is over, there is always a 'victor's fashion', and it is not only linked to dress. American lifestyles, for example, were imported to Europe after the Second World War and modern European culture owes much to the thought, art, music and cinema of its transatlantic ally.[7]

Today, however, it is increasingly difficult to single out a victor's fashion, since the global dimension of society makes appearance styles uniform and confused. Jeans are worn from equatorial Africa to China, Rasta braids may be seen in blond Scandinavian locks, Doc Martens on Italian schoolgirls and Rambo-style waistcoats on city dwellers everywhere as part of anti-snatch fashion. This universalization and decontextualization of clothing signs is typical of the contemporary social landscape and lends force to a commitment to rethink the aesthetics of war in terms other than the glamorous.

In such a context Benjamin's reflections on the relation between technology, war and Fascism still seem extremely relevant.[8] For Benjamin, Fascism tends to 'aestheticise political life' (Benjamin 1955: 46), since it must give voice to the masses without encroaching upon established property rights. The ideological apparatus of Fascism exists to produce cultural values that, nevertheless, have a forced coexistence with technology, and it is this which produces the tendency towards self-destruction in the Fascist 'aestheticization' of politics; in other words, the tendency towards war. Benjamin quotes Marinetti's manifesto on the war in Ethiopia, in which the beauty of war is asserted: through the use of arms the dominion of man over machine is guaranteed. War creates the dream of the 'metalisation of the human body' and 'new architecture' (1956: 47). At this point, Benjamin writes, the self-alienation of humanity 'has reached a level that allows it to experience its own annihilation as supreme aesthetic enjoyment' (1956: 48). Today any philosophy of culture should be diametrically opposed to such a cult of self-annihilation and be committed instead to thinking of the present not just in terms of appearances.

Notes

1. The foundation of the Franciscan Order in 1223 introduced precise dress codes based on modesty, humility and the image of "Francis and Poverty".

2. A pope who has been compared in elegance to Picasso, Puccini and Marcello Mastroianni.

3. A mask to hide identity, silent shoes, comfortably fitting clothes, etc.

4. The Katanga-style Milanese student militants in the 1960s are an exception: their balaclavas and parkas, while hiding face and body, also started a fashion fad.

6. (see Chapter 5).

5. Of course, in terms of their actual or emotive value, the objects we carry around (keys, for example) can themselves be 'corporeal', in that they are a kind of social prosthesis, or artificial limb.

6. Some of us may even remember the athlete Florence Griffith, who designed her own track outfits.

7. From a liberated Paris, *Vogue America* even published the creations of the great French couturiers.

8. His essay 'Art in the Age of Mechanical Reproducibility' came out in 1936, at a time when the writer was well aware of the significance of the military and cultural policies of both Fascism and Nazism.

14

Objects

There are some everyday items of clothing that manage, more than others, to impose themselves as emblematic of an atmosphere or a mood. They are different from garments that explicitly refer to a historical period or a style, for example, the parka or army boots. 'Atmospheric' objects transcend epochs and styles, leaving behind a taste of the cult that is attributed to them. They are usually objects that are not very prominent on a stylistic level, but they are connoted by social discourses, especially the discourses of the mass media. They are usually indispensable everyday items of clothing which, at a certain point in the history of fashion, emerge from their banality and become the most talked about object, the object to which we dedicate particular enthusiasm and attention, bordering on fetishism.

Women's stockings are undoubtedly among these objects. Having come out of the anonymity that has accompanied them for the last twenty years, women's' stockings seem to have taken the place in public imagery until recently reserved for the bra. There are TV commercials, newspaper advertisements and billboards dedicated to them and in the big cities there are shops selling just stockings.

Stockings have rediscovered the prestige and allure that surrounded them in the 1950s and 1960s when it seemed that a nice pair of legs depended entirely on a nice pair of stockings. In those days such a belief was easy to instil in the heads of buyers and admirers, since at the start of the 1950s mass-produced sheer stockings made their entrance onto the fashion scene, with the commercialization in Europe, as well as in the United States, of women's nylon stockings, which were affordable for those who would never have been able to buy silk stockings, not even artificial silk ones. Nylon stockings were invented around 1940 when silk was replaced by this new material, discovered by the American Wallace H. Carothers in the research laboratory of E.I. du Pont de Nemours & Co. in Wilmington, Delaware. It is said that the name 'nylon' comes from the initials of the first names of the five female chemists who were part of the research team: Nancy, Yvonne, Louella, Olivia and Nina. Five pairs of legs which, we presume, quickly changed from wearing silk to wearing this new material.

In 1900, 88 per cent of women's stockings were made of cotton (see Chapter 6), 11 per cent of wool and only 1 per cent of silk. Around 1929 silk or rayon stockings accounted for 99 per cent, mainly thanks to the advent of shorter skirts, allowing more leg to be shown; though never completely, as the 1920s fashion for black stockings demonstrates. The nylon revolution was not able to continue immediately: wartime rationing decreed that from 1941 all silk and nylon be used to manufacture parachutes, thus provoking what came to be known in England as the 'sock shock'.

Memories of those days were then filtered through the famous seamed stockings which, like a dream come true, moved from the cinema screen, where they were worn only by a few screen divas, to the streets and everyday life. Often it was a real struggle to achieve a straight line on not always perfect legs and sometimes, when women couldn't afford them, they pencilled the line on their bare legs. Next memories pass through advertisements on the first Italian television *Caroselli*[1] where shots of women clad from the knee down in silk and cotton were accompanied by approving whistles from Brylcreamed admirers on their scooters and a chorus of 'Nice legs!'. All thanks to stockings.

The fascination of silk stockings, however, was called in doubt by the onslaught of tights, adored by the first champions of the miniskirt but cursed by the male gaze. According to some theorists of this gaze, tights were to damage eroticism irreparably, that eroticism of which the suspender belt is the supreme vehicle. Indeed, the suspender belt is an object to which many, perhaps too many, honours have been dedicated. Giovanni Bottiroli in his short book dedicated to this garment (*Il reggicalze* 1995) sings it praises in an approach combining philosophy, cinema, theories of the image and personal taste. Above all, the author evokes the seductive function of stockings: the suspender belt seems only to hold up stockings so that they can be unhooked and slid slowly down the legs, following the logic of 'full' and 'empty' that governs the sex appeal of the erotic body.

A logic which has inversely led to an advertisement featuring a swarthy Antonio Banderas putting stockings on a blonde Valeria Mazza's legs. The ad draws attention to the supposed resistance of the stockings advertised, which, like love, do not ladder. The stockings in question are not chaste tights but hold-ups with a lace border, and so the object and act of dressing confirm the theory of full and empty: every hold-up is on the dangerous and metastable edge of either staying up or coming down, between clothing the leg and revealing the nude upper thigh.

The last frontier in the history of stockings, the last bulwark of female narcissism, hold-ups have not, however, undermined the power of tights, which are looking for new ways forward, new ways to make themselves loved. And they are succeeding, above all because of their unbeatable comfort and ability to be worn under any garment. It must be said that to reach this point they have tried everything: 'silk feel', micro-fibre, 'nude look', incorporated suspender belts, different colours, fake fabric, tartan …

In any case, stockings – whether they be hold-ups, tights, opaque or transparent – are slowly consolidating the veridicity of their aesthetic and practical value, with the help, naturally, of publicity campaigns. Apart from the fact that they are an item of clothing which covers a highly erotic part of the female body, stockings today represent the traces a woman leaves on her journey through the world. They have become female 'legs' not just metaphorically and not just from a male voyeuristic point of view, a wonderfully ironic example of which can be seen in Truffaut's *L'homme qui amait les femmes*. The ambiguity surrounding fashion and its languages lends itself to numerous possible interpretations, while critical awareness and irony help us to succumb to the charm of certain statements without believing in them too much.

On Susan Sarandon's head as Louise while she gets ready for her journey with Thelma, the foulard, an accessory slightly neglected by recent fashion, made a small come back. Perhaps because its modernity has always been understood, or perhaps because American women have never really stopped wearing it (to hide their rollers as they walk down the street?), the image of Louise with her high chignon held in a square of soft material makes us think back over the history of this object in the imagery of twentieth century fashion. Audrey Hepburn in *Sabrina*, Rita Hayworth in *Miss Sadie Thompson* and Kim Basinger in *9½ Weeks* all wear foulards: in the first two cases the fashion of the time 'backed up' this accessory, while in the 1980s it was only allowed the ironic and parodic role of a blindfold in an erotic game.

The foulard undoubtedly has a strong sexual connotation, despite the fact that it is usually associated with 'well-to-do' ladies. Perhaps it is the original silk material that distinguishes it, giving it a 'caressable' character. The word 'foulard' originally referred to a typical way of working silk, with probable origins in the Far East. Its meaning was later extended to describe a square (approximately 90 cm by 90 cm) of the same fabric printed with various colours and designs. Of French origin, from the 1920s to the 1960s the foulard was the work of illustrious designers, Hermes in particular.

The foulard is a typical female garment for which the practical use (to protect from the cold or wind, or to cover a *décolleté*) is of secondary importance to the fact of its being a symbol of style. You either love it or you hate it, there is no in-between. There are many other ways to protect yourself from the cold, if you use a foulard it is by choice. It is precisely this *haute couture* aspect of the classic foulard that made its significance as a fashion item disappear from the 1960s to the 1980s. 'Ladies with foulards' have always existed, however; proof of this is to be found in the statistics from Hermes which, between 1970 and 1990, sold 9,000,000 foulards worldwide, one every three minutes during the Christmas period in Paris alone.

It was, above all, the anti-fashion of the 1960s and 1970s which, rather than putting an end to the foulard, saw its revival in different materials and for different uses. For example, the *cachecol*, a rectangular scarf made of silk or wool wound loosely round the neck or tied in a large knot with the ends tucked inside the shirt; or the ascot, the wide tie fastened with a knot or a brooch. These objects were used by men and women alike. Who can forget the bandana, the cowboys' cotton kerchief, tied to the motorbike wing mirror in *Easy Rider*. In the 1990s the bandana made a comeback with the young, worn not only round the neck but also on the head, pirate-style, tied round the waist like a belt, or tucked inside the waistcoat pocket. And a number of 'spurious' female uses for the classic silk foulard were introduced in the 1980s: for example, as a shawl over the coat, or over the swimming costume like a small *pareu*, an essential part of the game of transparencies on the body.

In the context of global textile production, the phenomenon of fakes is spreading: Taiwan, the Philippines and various eastern countries have become workshops where famous designs are copied onto silk or cotton foulards, or new ones are invented. Many famous fashion houses even allow some of these factories to use their label, thereby creating that strange admixture of 'authentic' and 'fake' in which is contained the atypical status of today's fashion items in terms of their market and aesthetic value. A status which includes the unique, absolutely luxurious value of a foulard from a collection, like many famous articles by Hermes, or like the *mouchoir illustré* by Buquet whose tradition goes back to the nineteenth century.

According to Simmel the fascination of fashion lies, amongst other things, in its ability to make everyone feel part of a social circle, without denying the possibility of adding a personal touch. If the worldly nature of fashion has modified Simmel's analysis somewhat, having made fashion a 'universally individual' language, objects like the foulard can be taken as a small exception which generates both social 'closure' and a personal touch.

It is not unusual for the vocabulary of fashion to borrow terms and expressions from other 'specialized languages'. In this case the Italian word for bum-bag, *marsupio*, has been plundered from zoological vocabulary where, as we know, it refers to the abdominal pouch in which the females of certain mammals (known as marsupials) keep their young. The analogy between the pouch used by kangaroos and koala bears and these bags, closed with a zip and fastened round the waist, containing money and documents, stops however at the fact that both are containers situated on the abdomen. Greater functional and aesthetic analogies can be drawn between the animal pouch and the padded cloth 'pouches' used to carry human babies in 'primitive' and, more recently, in metropolitan societies.

The bum-bag is predominantly practical in origin: we can trace it back to those little bags of various shapes and sizes which have always existed for soldiers, hunters, fishermen, mountaineers and other sportsmen, in which they keep arms, ammunition, snap-links, bait and other small objects. From the military or sporting uniform to fashion is but a short step, and so the bum-bag, as it is commonly known in English, has become an accessory used by the most disparate types. From travellers who need a safe place to keep money and documents, to women afraid of bag snatchers, from hikers who want to leave their hands and pockets free, to kids who have finally got somewhere to keep their chewing gum, pocket money, lucky charms and football stickers.

In recent years the bum-bag has changed from a sports items, produced in more or less standard colours and models, to an accessory available in shops selling leather goods; or it may be made of luxury fabrics for special occasions. The original sports bum-bags, on the other hand, have increased their range of styles and colours. Now they are available in double nylon, pile, rough materials like jute, and in a selection of gaudy colours, but also in leather and suede, natural tones, gold or silver, or decorated with sequins or studs. There are also models in different shapes and sizes: oval, triangular, rectangular, with open and closed pockets, made to hold not only a wallet but also sunglasses, keys, credit cards, pens, mobile phones and cameras.

It is important, however, that the bum-bag have a solid belt and a safe buckle to avoid being snatched. In big cities, where people are most at risk from theft, it seems that bum-bags are safer than pockets or shoulder bags, because it is more difficult to rip or pull them away from the waist. Moreover, the smaller models can comfortably be hidden under jackets and coats, except that they compromise your figure, which seems a little bigger round the waist. A small price to pay for safety!

Above all, the bum-bag seems to be an accessory for people who do a lot of walking. Together with a small backpack and roller-blades, it makes up the uniform of mostly young people who love to streak along as fast as possible on their own two feet. The bum-bag goes well with trainers, too, from the most exaggerated ones, with flashing lights or compressed air, so loved by teenagers, to the more normal ones, comfortable just the same and made for ploughing along the tarmac, or at least for giving that impression. So, those who use a bum-bag walk, or so it would seem. Apart from anything else, they are uncomfortable to wear for hours in the car or sitting down.

As mentioned above, the etymology of the Italian name for this object, *marsupio*, is the animal marsupial pouch, where the young complete their growth. It is an extension of the mother's belly which the young cannot do without. It is not simply a metaphor for growth as a journey ... In many societies, including our own, mothers and fathers carry their children on their stomachs, as in a marsupial pouch, or on their backs, in a kind of backpack, wherever they go.

At the beginning of the twenty-first century our bum-bags, in which we seem to keep everything, contribute to the construction of a new kind of *flâneur* (or *flâneuse*) who, after a century of sleep, is rediscovering the street as a place full of life, culture and civilization, and is, moreover, reviving the image of the mother walking with her offspring (all that she has) glued to her body. We are left with the question whether the almost automatic journey on which we are led (wearing our bum-bags, naturally) inevitably means that we will get lost, or whether, even though we are con-fused in the crowd, indeed precisely because we are so confused and have come so far, we will somehow find our way.

'Stand up straight!', 'Shoulders back!': the deadly chant continues to res-onate in the ears of many children persecuted by their parents' and teachers' fears because of their loose gaits and the strange positions of their backs, sure-fire ways of developing terrible back problems. It is useless for doctors and specialists to repeat that it is indeed important for teenagers to adopt a correct posture, but that it is even more important for them to do physical exercise in order to guarantee correct growth.

The most recent worry over young backs concerns the rucksack, or better, a rucksack full of books, the weight of which distresses parents and school workers every academic year. Children with rucksacks on their backs are a common sight on our streets. Older and younger children are brought together by this distinctive sign, which has taken the place of folders or the straps once used to hold books together.

The history of the mass diffusion of this object is not very recent: since the 1960s and 1970s, before filling classrooms, the rucksack had become the required suitcase substitute for round-the-world travellers and back-packers. Who can forget stations, ports and airports before the advent of suitcases on wheels? Initially the models were much less imaginative: there was the military version, often bought at the army surplus store, and there was the 'anatomical' version with a metal frame that was supposed to support it and keep it close to your body without causing back problems (though it was actually incredibly uncomfortable to wear).

The origins of the rucksack are twofold: military and alpine. Both soldiers and mountaineers have always needed a bag in which they could keep things, while leaving their hands free to carry a rifle or grasp a safe hold, depending on the situation. Carrying heavy loads on the shoulders is a feature of many societies and cultures, in everyday situations which have nothing to do with wars or mountains. Think of the peasants' use of panniers, bundles and sacks; or the tradition of the American Indians who carry their children on their backs in a piece of material folded like a kind of rucksack (called a papoose). This custom has been adopted by companies in the West that specialize in baby products and that now make rucksacks for carrying children.

Today rucksacks (whether for travel, school, the motorbike or the mountains) have multiplied in shape, size and colour, as well as in their adaptations and transformations, like those with a walkman incorporated. The better brands are distinguished by their ergonomic and functional nature: they have extra-light anatomical skeletons, are made of resistant, waterproof materials, or fabrics which absorb sweat, with internal and external pockets, a belt to fasten round the hips to help support the weight, and straps made to carry snap-links, flasks, sleeping bags or walking boots. These are all factors which have contributed to the success of the rucksack and which allow many people, not just the young, to use this object in a personalized way and yet to feel part of a group. The rucksack has become another of those 'multiform uniforms' that characterize our age, a symbol of cult and culture at the same time. The fact that it may contain a Greek dictionary, a waterproof jacket or a snack is simply indicative of one of the desires that characterize our age: to be able to carry on our shoulders everywhere something like Mary Poppins' never-ending bag.

The beret has never stopped being worn by young and old, male and female alike, in many parts of the world. Typical of the *time of fashion* is the idea of eternal return, the cyclical nature of which presents objects from the past as if they were new and had never been seen before. In the 1990s the beret changed its size and, especially in the female version, became brightly coloured; and it was worn like the painter's beret, or else in the centre of the head to cover the hair completely. The rule was: once you wear it, never take it off, keep it on your head in the restaurant, at your friends' house, in the cinema and even in the classroom.

This kind of head covering has a long history: its origins can be traced back to the ancient Greeks and Romans, when it was held on by a wide band, which can still be seen on some versions, but which is absent on those known as the *modelaine*. The bobble, an essential feature in most models, is what remains of the original cover over the central hole. Around the end of the nineteenth century women's berets were decorated with feathers, flowers and ribbons, which were then abandoned a few decades later in the version made famous by Greta Garbo in her beige overcoat, part Mata Hari, part Ninotschka. A beret with a pom-pom and a long pheasant's feather was worn once again by Katherine Hepburn as Mary Queen of Scots in the film *Mary of Scotland* by John Ford.

Like certain other garments, the beret epitomizes the changing relationship between fashion items and military clothing. We can see this in the berets of the fashion house Kangol, one of the main producers of this garment, which was founded in England in 1938. It supplied the British armed forces during the Second World War and was very successful in European boutiques in the 1950s, a success which was renewed in the 1990s thanks to collaboration with the designer Graham Smith. Although it is alarming to think that war is often the inspiration for fashion, the civilian contamination of uniforms does sometimes work as an irreverent parody of perfect men in their perfect outfits.

The beret is an item of military clothing with more than one meaning: it evokes the uniforms worn by special forces, like the 'green berets', whose warlike vocation is well known, and peace-keeping forces like the UN 'blue berets', the colour of which links them symbolically to peace missions. During both Gulf Wars, seen through television coverage, there was always a beret stuck sideways on Saddam Hussein's head, but also the British general, who was likened to Montgomery for his icy aplomb, wore a beret. The large, black, leather-trimmed beret used by the paramilitary appears on the heads of dubious subjects, a sublime parody of which is seen in the hysterical and decidedly Nazi-like student who is the butt of a witty vendetta at the hands of John Belushi in *Animal House*.

For the generations of 'anti-fashion' in the 1960s and 1970s the beret was predominantly a close fitting, dark blue one with a red star on the front, like that of Che Guevara. And many continue to wear a similar version today. With the recent rediscovery of Che, his mythology and twentieth century Latin American history, the Guevara or Sandinista beret has made a comeback, often worn with an earring or a Palestinian kefiyah.

A socio-linguistic reflection on the word for this garment seems called for here: in the English-speaking world the French word 'beret' is used, while Italians use the word 'basco', which comes from the 'Basque' country, where this garment is widely used and where it is a symbol of nationalism and autonomy. An identical custom may be seen in some parts of France and Italy; in Sardinia, for example, where local tradition merges with deep-seated political, often socialist, tradition.

From Faye Dunaway in *Bonnie and Clyde* to Madonna, from Salvator Dalì to English boarding school pupils, the list of those who wear a beret is never ending, in a game of cross-references, citations and models which exist in our minds without our knowing it. Thus the power of certain fashion items to transform a classic into a cult is confirmed.

'Scarperentola' (from the Italian for 'shoe' – 'scarpa' – and 'Cinderella' – 'Cenerentola') was a show in Milan at the beginning of the 1990s dedicated to shoes, which brought together artists and designers from all over the world. In it shoes were presented not only as canonical items for the feet, but also as items of furniture, ornaments, armchairs and so on, in accordance with the popular tendency ('postmodern' or 'neobaroque' depending on one's point of view) to take an object out of its appointed place and have it fulfil another role. The play on words which inspired the title of the show underlines the link between shoes and fairytales – that is, between daily life and social imagery – forged through the universally recognizable character of Cinderella in her various guises, and, by contrast, the fact that the shoe is only the seeming 'Cinderella' of clothing.

Indeed, compared to the ugly step sisters, represented in a narrow sense by clothing, shoes, which are commonly defined as 'accessories', have known various forms of resurgence, becoming important objects both in the search for stylistic novelty and in the public's attention, at different times in the history of costume and fashion. Our era seems to be one of these moments. An indicator of this recent transformation can be found in the world of shoe advertising, where we can see a change of emphasis from 'adventure shoes' and 'comfortable shoes' to the possibility of giving the shoe its own specific 'language' which is not directly tied to function.

Luciana Boccardi (1993) says something similar, from the point of view of the 'internal' history of the shoe, stating that shoes began to catalyse the creativity of designers in the 1990s and to gain an important position on the commercial market and in the world of fashion. Boccardi concentrates on women's evening footwear, or party shoes. Yet she also writes a full history of this object, in which she maintains that, apart from their changing aesthetics, shoes have always fulfilled a symbolic role: for example, in the seventeenth century shoes 'in the French style' or 'in the Spanish style' expressed political preferences; dancing shoes in the period leading up to the First World War epitomized the philosophy of 'flaunting not hiding' typical of fashion in those years; the 'flower children' in the 1960s danced barefoot or in Indian sandals, taken from the culture that had inspired their movement.

It is certainly true that the shoe has a special symbolic function: the story of Cinderella is itself a metaphor, whereby the shoe, according to one widely accepted anthropological-psychoanalytical interpretation, represents the young girl's rite of passage from puberty to sexual maturity. Yet Cinderella's shoe is also a garment whose identity is established a priori: the shoe fits her and only her, with no pity for the cruel stepsisters, one of whom even cuts off part of her foot to make it fit, but in vain. This says a lot about the normative function of fairytales for both children and grown-ups.

In the same way a lot can be said about the relation between shoes and identity: the word 'shoe' may even indicate a social or hierarchical role, as in the phrase 'to put yourself in someone else's shoes'. In the fairytale *The Red Shoes* the rather sadistic Hans Christian Andersen makes the main character pay, with the amputation of her feet, for the sin of wanting to wear red shoes, like the king's daughter, on the day of her Confirmation, instead of sober black ones. Indeed, when she puts on the forbidden shoes she is at first swept away in an unstoppable St Vitus' Dance and then her feet are themselves transformed into shoes, which is why she has to resort to cutting them off and ends her days in a convent. The moral of the story is clearly that everyone should stay 'in their own shoes'. Perhaps after reading it these objects, which are a fetish for many people and of which many have entire collections, seem less tantalizing.

In the West we are shocked by the oriental custom of foot-binding. Yet this custom is one of many ritual techniques which reshape the body through using articles of clothing, be they the necklaces of the African 'giraffe women', earrings to lengthen earlobes, corsets in the nineteenth century, or the skin-tight jeans and narrow shoes we use today.[2]

Stilettos have populated the imagery of fashion in successive waves, which recently has been invaded by an explicit fetish for high heels, as high and thin as possible. They represent an object with an irresistible appeal, even though it is now well known that their prolonged use leads to severe arthritis of the knee. Amongst the explanations for this preference there is one which seems particularly interesting: stilettos give an unstable gait to the woman wearing them, a gait which assumes a different cast, depending on the pressure exerted by different body types on feet in high heels. In this way a synergy is created between the body and the garment, between the organic and the inorganic, a synergy which has a unique attraction. Is this an over-intellectual explanation, or merely an attempt to detect the important link between body signs and sensory perception through a fashion item?

Despite their being what is usually referred to as accessories, the fact remains that shoes are a symbol of the utmost importance, both because of their role in the history of costume and because of their collocation in the hierarchy of fashion values. In an advertisement a few years ago, a pair of pure white trainers became the 'page' upon which a charming, noble oriental lover left his mark after a night of passion with the traveller who owned the shoes. When she arrived home the proud girl washed her shoes in the washing machine and erased the sign. Now back to normal, the shoes were ready to accompany her on new journeys, new adventures. Perhaps this is what we want from a pair of shoes: that they accompany us, whether we share the slightly perverse desires of a *dominatrix* in stilettos, or whether we believe in the happiness that a pair of shoes can give us, in the essentialness of a comfortable pair of flat shoes, the sturdiness of a pair of Clarks or the aggressiveness of a pair of military boots. To accompany us even in conflicts, in moments of disharmony, or in the pleasant imperfections which an unexpected juxtaposition can create.

In the novel *L'amant* the main character speaks of a pair of gold lamé high-heeled shoes, bought in the sales for her by her mother. These are the only shoes she can wear on every occasion, the only shoes in which she can bear to see herself, precisely because of the strange effect they create, like her broad-brimmed man's hat. The image is suggestive: how to oppose nature with a sign that has no exchange value, is not even useful, but that has a great aesthetic and communicative value, enough to transcend stereotypes.

Perhaps it is precisely the relation between shoes and identity that makes this item interesting again today, in an age when aesthetic choices, in the sense of choices profoundly linked to human feeling, convey behavioural patterns, aspirations and values. So, on the long journey they have to make, shoes certainly outstrip our feet.

In the film *Le bonheur est dans le pré* being able to wear a pair of trainers with a shirt and tie represents one of the cardinal points of this 'happiness'. The trainers are those bulky ones made of rubber and leather, with a high, well-turned sole, equipped with the little symbol or customary label; shoes which, for some time, have taken over the feet of a growing number of people of all ages, though it is mainly teenagers who choose them for their everyday *look*.

Perhaps we are attracted by the advertisements, showing demons playing football, sports champions competing against lions, balls thrown between cities, or slogans carved in stone encouraging us to act. We are also attracted by the exceptional comfort of this type of footwear. Teenagers worldwide walk the streets wearing trainers. You need only wait half an hour at the entrance to any school or university and look down at the feet of pupils or students to see how much tarmac is trodden by trainers, which are no longer simply functional sports objects, but great containers of everyday stories, symbols of belonging to a style, banners of a certain world view; they are shoes that go beyond fashion, while remaining a part of it.

Experimentation in the manufacture of sports shoes launches itself into ever more complicated projects which correspond to a price increase seemingly at odds with the widespread success of this footwear. The foot can float on air bubbles contained in the sole, which in some cases can be adjusted with a little pump, sweat can be extracted by an intelligent and ingenious ventilation system, and some of the materials are the same as those used by NASA. Technology and *look* are united once again, and it matters little where one ends and the other begins.

The mechanism by which this sturdy footwear has found its way into the everyday wardrobe of people worldwide is not very different from that which, during the twentieth century, blessed the spread of jeans beyond the workplaces for which they were originally designed. Nevertheless, it would be premature to risk hypotheses on how long this particular fashion will last and it is clear that the success of jeans is unique.

Launched by images coming from American television, as well as by a kind of worldwide smoke-signalling, the fashion for wearing trainers on every occasion comes from the consolidated habit of transferring sports clothes to everyday contexts. Particularly amongst the young, who don't need to wear a 'uniform' to work, casual clothing represents 'freedom', even though such freedom of dress is nevertheless controlled by a tacit group approval. This is an almost automatic mechanism according to which, for example, every teenager who wears trainers with a certain trademark can relax in the knowledge that there is a community of peers who will approve of them, admire them and even want to imitate them.

Undoubtedly, the trainers that are around these days, with their huge, heavy shapes and sometimes excessive designs, would have made the same sports gear worshippers screw up their noses until just a few years ago. Trainers were considered sober and functional: who can forget the traditional blue and white trainers worn strictly in the 'right' circumstances, that is, for training, jogging or going to the gym? Tennis shoes began to take some liberties in the 1970s on the wave of the worldly eccentricity and wealth of tennis champions. It was still a matter of elegance, however, limited to selected places. The finishing touch to the shape of sports shoes undoubtedly came from basketball, particularly American basketball, which has always been spectacular, its popularity based on athletic excellence and technical experimentation, including experimentation in sports clothing. Metropolitan life styles, too, where walking is sometimes the only sport available, have contributed to the spread and decontextualization of trainers.

If, then, for teenagers, wearing these shoes is a way of keeping alive a kind of pack spirit, for adults it is a (perhaps unwitting) attempt to bring free time into the sedentary, monotonous workplace, to bring an imaginary flash of green lanes into cramped, badly lit workplaces, to find, in an almost metonymic way, happiness in a shoe.

Notes

1. A popular children's television programme in Italy from the 1960s.

2. In an imaginary mega-shoe shop first, in honour of Cinderella, we see her glass slippers which, rather than being made of glass, are actually made of satin and velvet; then we see the stilettos worn by Anita Ekberg in *La Dolce Vita*; then the ballet slippers made fashionable by Isadora Duncan; the zigzag *décolleté* Marinetti imagined for his ideal woman; American Indian leather moccasins; Roman sandals; platforms from the 1930s, 1970s and 1990s; discreet Chanel models; Tod's with 133 heels; cricket shoes by Hogan; oriental *babouches*; Dr Martens.

Bibliography

Arendt, Hanna (1982), *Lectures on Kant's Political Philosophy*, It. tr. by P.P. Portinaro, *Teoria del giudizio politico*, Genova: Il Melangolo, 1990.

Ash, Juliet and Wilson, Elizabeth (1993), *Chic Thrills*, Berkeley and Los Angeles: California University Press.

Aumont, Jacques (1998), *A cosa pensano i film*, intervista a c. di N. Dusi, "Segno cinema", anno XVIII, n. 92.

Aumont, Jacques *et al.* (1994), *Estetica del film*, Torino: Lindau, 1995.

Bakhtin, Mikhail (1965), *Tvorcestvo Fransua Rable i narodnaya kultura srednevekovya i Renessansa*, It. tr. by M. Romano, *L'opera di Rabelais e la cultura popolare*, Torino: Einaudi, 1979.

Barthes, Roland (1957), *Mythologies*, It. tr. by L. Lonzi, *Miti d'oggi*, Torino: Einaudi, 1974.

—— (1967), *Système de la Mode*, Eng. tr. *The Fashion System*, Berkeley: University of California Press, 1990.

—— (1970), *L'empire des signes*, It. tr. by M. Vallora, *L'impero dei segni*, Torino: Einaudi, 1984.

—— (1975), *Introduzione alla "Fisiologia del gusto" di Brillat Savarin*, Palermo: Sellerio, 1978.

—— (1977), *Fragments d'un discours amoureux*, Paris: Seuil, It. tr. by R. Guidieri, *Frammenti di un discorso amoroso*, Torino: Einaudi, 1979.

—— (1981), *Le grain del la voix*, It. tr. by L. Lonzi, *La grana della voce*, Torino: Einaudi, 1986.

—— (1982), *L'obvie et l'obtus. Essais critiques III*, It. tr. by C. Benincasa, G. Bottiroli, G.P. Caprettini, D. De Agostini, L. Lonzi, G. Mariotti, *L'ovvio e l'ottuso. Saggi critici III*, Torino: Einaudi, 1985.

—— (1984), *Le bruissement de la langue. Essais critiques IV*, It. tr. by B. Bellotto, *Il brusio della lingua*, Torino: Einaudi, 1988.

—— (1998), *Scritti. Società, testo, comunicazione*, ed. G. Marrone, Torino: Einaudi.

Barzini, Benedetta (1993), *Storia di una passione senza corpo*, Milano, Frassinelli.

Bataille, Georges (1973), *L'experience interieur*, It. tr. by C. Morena, *L'esperienza interiore*, Bari: Dedalo, 1978.

Baudelaire, Charles (1863), "La peintre de la vie moderne", It. tr. and ed. by G. Guglielmi and E. Raimondi, "Il pittore della vita moderna", in *Scritti sull'arte*, Torino: Einaudi, 1981.

Baudrillard, Jean (1976), *L'échange symbolique et la mort*, It. tr. by G. Mancuso, *Lo scambio simbolico e la morte*, Milano: Feltrinelli, 1979.

Benjamin, Walter (1931), *Il carattere distruttivo*, in AA.VV., *Il carattere distruttivo. L'orrore del quotidiano*, "Millepiani", 4, Milano: Mimesis, 1995.
—— (1955), *Das Kunstwerk im Zeitalter seiner Reproduzierbarkeit*, It. tr. by E. Filippini, *L'opera d'arte nell'epoca della sua riproducibilità tecnica*, Torino: Einaudi, 1966.
—— (1982), *Das Passagen Werk* [1927–1940], ed. R. Tiedemann, It. ed. G. Agamben, It. tr. by R. Solmi, A. Moscati, M. De Carolis, G. Russo, G. Garchia, F. Porzio, *Parigi, capitale del XIX secolo*, Torino: Einaudi, 1986.
Benveniste, Emile (1969), *Il vocabolario delle istituzioni indoeuropee*, Torino: Einaudi, 1976.
Boccardi, Luciana (1993), *Le scarpe delle feste*, Modena: Zanfi.
Bogatyrëv, Pëtr (1937),"Funkcie kroja na moravskom Slovensku", It. tr. by R. Bruzzese, "La funzioni dell'abbigliamento popolare nella Slovacchia morava", in *Semiotica della cultura popolare*, ed. M. Solimini, Verona: Bertani, 1983.
Bottiroli, Giovanni (1995), *Il reggicalze*, Torino: Gribaudo.
Bruzzi, Stella (1997), *Clothing and Identity in the Movies*, London and New York: Routledge.
Butler, Judith (1990), *Gender Trouble. Feminism and the Subversion of Identity*, New York and London, Routledge.
Cadigan, Pat (1990), 'Fool to Believe', It.tr. 'Chi credi di essere?' in P. Nicolazzini, (ed.) *Cyberpunk*, Milano: Editrice Nord.
Calabrese, Omar, *Lo stile degli stilisti*, in Calefato 1992.
Calefato, Patrizia (1986), *Il corpo rivestito*, Bari: Ed. dal Sud.
—— (1988), 'Fashion, the passage, the body', *Cultural Studies* 2(2).
—— (ed.) (1992a), *Moda & mondanità*, Bari: Palomar.
—— (1992b), 'Proper names in the symbolic economy of fashion', *Semiotica* 91(1/2).
—— (1993), 'Pop Model', in Calefato, Ceriani & Pozzato 1993.
—— (1994), *Europa fenicia*, Milano: Angeli.
—— (1996), *Mass moda*, Genova: Costa & Nolan.
—— (1997a), 'Fashion and worldliness: language and imagery of the clothed body', *Fashion Theory* 1(1).
—— (1997b), *Sociosemiotica*, Bari: Graphis.
—— (ed.) (1999), *Moda e cinema. Macchine di senso/scritture del corpo*, Milano and Genova: Costa & Nolan.
—— (2002), *Segni di moda*, Bari: Palomar.
—— (2003), *Lusso*, Roma: Meltemi.
——, Ceriani, Giulia and Pozzato, Maria Pia (1993), *La Moda: analisi semiotiche*, Documenti di lavoro e pre-pubblicazioni del Centro internazionale di Semiotica e di Linguistica, Università di Urbino, no. 224–5.
Capucci, Pier Luigi (ed.) (1994), *Il corpo tecnologico*, Bologna: Baskerville.
Caronia, A. (1994), *Wired*, testo in circolazione telematica su "One-net".
Castelnuovo, Vittorio (1994), 'Hip', in Perniola 1994.
Ceriani, Giulia and Grandi, Roberto (ed.) (1995), *Moda: regole e rappresentazioni*, Milano: Angeli.
Chambers, Iain (1985), *Urban Rhythms*, It. tr. by P. Prato, *Ritmi urbani*, Genova:

Costa & Nolan, 1987.

—— (1994), *Migrancy, Culture, Identity*, London and New York: Routledge.

—— (2003), *Paesaggi migratori*, Roma: Meltemi.

Chatwin, Bruce (1987), *The Songlines*, It. tr. by S. Gariglio, *Le vie dei canti*, Milano: Adelphi, 1988.

Colaizzi, Giulia (1995), "Il ciborghesco, o del grottesco tecnologico", in stampa in Calefato, P. (ed.), *Scritture/Visioni*, Bari: Ed. Dal Sud, 1996.

—— (1999), 'Il "camp": travestimento e identità', in Calefato 1999.

Damisch, Hubert (1979), 'Maschera', in *Enciclopedia*, vol. 8, Torino: Einaudi.

Daniel, Tony (1992), 'Death of Reason', It. tr. 'Morte della ragione' in P. Nicolazzini (ed.), *Cyberpunk*, Milano: Editrice Nord, 1992.

Devlin, Polly (1979), *Vogue. Book of Fashion Photography*, It. tr. by F. Saba Sardi, *Vogue 1920–1980. Moda, immagine, costume*, Milano: Fabbri, 1980.

Duras, Marguerite (1984), *L'amant*, It. tr. by L. Prata Caruso, *L'amante*, Milano: Feltrinelli, 1985.

El Guindi, Fadwa (1999a), *Veil*, Oxford: Berg, 1999.

—— (1999b), 'Veiling resistance', *Fashion Theory*, 3(1), 51–80.

El-Houssi, Majid (1987), 'La vision islamique du voile', *Lectures* 20.

Enzensberger, Hans Magnus (1993), "La morte della moda", *La Stampa*, 17 September.

European Commission (1995), *Green Paper on Innovation*, COM(95)688.

Faludi, Susan (1992), *Contrattacco*, Milano: Baldini & Castoldi.

Fashion Theory, The Journal of Dress, Body & Culture, ed. Valerie Steele, vols. 1–3, 1997–9, Oxford: Berg.

Foucault, Michel (1975), *Surveiller et punir. Naissance de la prison*, It. tr. by A. Tarchetti, *Sorvegliare e punire. Nascita della prigione*, Torino: Einaudi, 1978.

—— (1976), *La volonté de savoir*, It. tr. by P. Pasquino and G. Procacci, *La volontà di sapere. Storia della sessualità 1*, Milano: Feltrinelli, 1978.

—— (1977), *Microfisica del potere*, ed. A. Fontana and P. Pasquino, Torino: Einaudi.

Gandelman, Claude (1992), 'Moda e testualità', in Calefato 1992.

Gelas, Nadine (1992), "Moda e linguaggio: quando la moda si serve delle parole", in Calefato 1992.

Gibson, William (1984), *Neuromancer*, It. tr. by G. Cossato and S. Sandrelli, *Neuromante*, Milano: Editrice Nord, 1991.

Gilroy, Paul (1992), *The Black Atlantic: Modernity and Double Consciousness*, Cambridge, MA: Harvard University Press.

Gramsci, Antonio (1975), *Quaderni del carcere*, ed. V. Gerratana, Torino: Einaudi.

Greimas, Algirdas Julien (1970), *Del senso*, Milano: Bompiani, 1974

—— (1976), *Semiotica e scienze sociali* (1976), Torino: Centro Scientifico Editore, 1991.

—— (1983), *Del senso 2. Narrativa, modalità, passioni*, Milano: Bompiani, 1984.

—— (1987), *Dell'imperfezione*, Palermo: Sellerio, 1988.

—— (1995), *L'imperfezione e l'estasi*, Conversazione a c. di N. Tasca and C. Zilberberg, in G. Marrone (ed. by) *Sensi e discorso*, Bologna: Progetto Leonardo.

Grisham, John (1992), *Il rapporto Pelican*, Milano: Mondadori, 1992.

Haraway, Donna (1991), *Simians, Cyborgs, and Women*, New York: Routledge.
—— (1995), *Manifesto Cyborg*, ed. L. Borghi, Milano: Feltrinelli, 1995.
Hebdige, Dick(1979), *Subculture: the Meaning of Style*, It. tr. by P. Tazzi, *Sottocultura: il fascino di uno stile innaturale*, Genova: Costa & Nolan, 1983.
Heidegger, Martin (1977), *Vier Seminare*, Frankfurt am Main: Vittorio Klostermann.
Hjelmslev, Louis (1961), *Prolegomena to a Theory of Language*, Madison: University of Wisconsin Press.
hooks, bell (1990), *Yearning. Race, Gender, and Cultural Politics*, Boston: South End Press.
—— (1998), *Elogio del margine*, Milano: Feltrinelli, 1998.
Jakobson, Roman (1963), *Saggi di linguistica generale*, Milano: Feltrinelli 1981.
Jayadeva, *Gitagovinda*, ed. G. Bolcali, Milano: Adelphi, 1982.
Kaiser, Susan (1992), "La politica e l'estetica dello stile delle apparenze", in Calefato 1992.
Kant, Immanuel, *Kritik der Urteilskraft*, It. tr. by A. Gargiulo, ed. V. Verra, *Critica del giudizio*, Roma and Bari: Laterza, 1982.
Klossowski, Pierre (1970), *La Monnaie Vivante* , It. tr. R. Chiurco, *La moneta vivente*, Milano: Mimesis, 1989.
Kristeva, Julia (1969), Shmeiwtich. *Recherches pour une sémanalyse*, It. tr. by P. Ricci, Shmeiwtich. *Ricerche per una semanalisi*, Milano: Feltrinelli, 1978.
Lauretis, Teresa de (1987), *Technologies of Gender*, Bloomington and Indianapolis: Indiana University Press.
—— (1997), *Pratica d'amore. Percorsi del desiderio perverso*, Milano: La Tartaruga.
Lee, Martyn J. (1993), 'La "fluidizzazione" del consumo', in E. Di Nallo (ed.), *Il significato sociale del consumo*, Roma and Bari, Laterza, 1997.
Leopardi, Giacomo, *Dialogo della Moda e della Morte*, in *Operette morali* (1827), ed. S. Solmi, Torino: Einaudi Classici Ricciardi, 1976.
Levi Pisetzky, Rosita (1978), *Il costume e la moda nella società italiana*, Torino: Einaudi.
Lévinas, Emmanuel (1979), *La traccia dell'altro*, Napoli: Libreria Tullio Pironti.
Lévi-Strauss, Claude (1958), *Anthropologie structurale*, It. tr. by P. Caruso, *Antropologia strutturale*, Milano: Il Saggiatore, 1966, 1980.
—— (1962), *Le pensèe sauvage*, It. tr. by P. Caruso, *Il pensiero selvaggio*, Milano: Il Saggiatore, 1964.
Liperi, Felice (1988), 'Tecnoribellione. Oltre il fascino della musica', *Gomorra* 1.
Lipovetski, Gilles (1987), *L'empire de l'éphèmere*, Paris: Gallimard.
Lotman, Juri M, (1993), *Kul'tura i Vzryv*, It. tr. by C. Valentino, *La cultura e l'esplosione*, Milano: Feltrinelli.
Lurie, Alison (1981), *The Language of Clothes*, New York: Vintage Books.
Marrone, Gianfranco (1995) (ed.), *Sensi e discorso*, Bologna: Progetto Leonardo.
—— (1998), 'Introduzione' to R. Barthes, *Scritti. Società, testo, comunicazione*, Torino: Einaudi, 1998.
—— (2001), *Corpi sociali*, Torino: Einaudi.
Martin, Richard (1998), 'A note: Gianni Versace's anti-bourgeois little black dress (1994)', *Fashion Theory*, 2(2).

—— and Wilkes, Andrew (1998), 'Cine/moda', in *Moda/cinema*, Catalogo della Mostra della Biennale di Firenze, Milano: Electa.

Marx, Karl (1844), *Ökonomisch-philosophische Manuskripte aus dem Jahre 1844*, It. tr. by G. Della Volpe, *Manoscritti economico-filosofici del 1844*, in *Opere filosofiche giovanili*, Roma: Editori Riuniti, 1971[4].

—— (1867), *Das Kapital*, It. tr. by D. Cantimori, *Il capitale*, libro I, Roma: Editori Riuniti, 1970.

McCracken, Grant (1988), 'Il potere evocativo delle cose', in E. Di Nallo (ed.), *Il significato sociale del consumo*, Roma and Bari: Laterza, 1997.

McDermott, Catherine (1987), *Street Style. British Design in the 80s*, London: The Design Council.

Molho, Renata (1998), 'Riflessioni', in *Moda/cinema*, Catalogo della Mostra della Biennale di Firenze, Milano: Electa.

Moltedo, Adriana (1998) (ed.), *Pelle di donna. Moda e bellezza*, Roma: Stampa alternativa.

Morris, Charles (1964), "Signification and Significance", It. tr. by S. Petrilli, "Significazione e significatività", in *Segni e valori*, Bari: Adriatica 1988.

Mulvey, Laura (1989), *Visual and Other Pleasures*, Bloomington and Indianapolis, Indiana University Press.

Museo Salvatore Ferragamo (1998), *Cenerentola*, Milano: Electa, Biennale di Firenze.

Negroponte, Nicholas (1995), *Being Digital*, It. tr. by F. and G. Filippazzi, *Essere digitali*, Milano: Sperling & Kupfer, 1995.

O'Hara, Georgina (1986), *The Encyclopaedia of fashion*, It. tr. by R. Panuzzo and J. Valli, *Il dizionario della moda*, Bologna: Zanichelli, 1990.

Pastoreau, Michel (1991), *L'etoffe du Diable*, It. tr. by M. Scotti, *La stoffa del diavolo*, Genova: Il Melangolo, 1993.

Perniola, Mario (1988) (ed.), *Estetica News* 3, "Moda e mondanità".

—— (1990), *Enigmi. Il momento egizio nella società e nell'arte*, Genova: Costa & Nolan.

—— (1994a), *Il sex-appeal dell'inorganico*, Torino: Einaudi.

—— (1994b) (ed.), *L'aria si fa tesa*, Genova: Costa & Nolan.

Piccinini, Laura (1991), 'C'è un generale nel mio armadio', *Il Manifesto*, 9 February.

Poe, Edgar Allan (1840), *The Man of the Crowd*, It. tr. by G. Sardelli and M. Gallone, *L'uomo della folla*, in *Racconti del mistero e dell'orrore. Arabeschi*, Milano: Sugarco, 1974.

Polhemus, Ted (1994), *Street Style*, London: Thames & Hudson.

—— (1996), *Style Surfing*, London: Thames & Hudson.

—— and Procter, Lynn (1978), *Fashion & Anti-fashion*, London: Thames & Hudson.

Ponzio, Augusto (1995), *I segni dell'altro*, Napoli: ESI.

—— (1997), *Elogio dell'infunzionale*, Roma: Castelvecchi.

—— (1997), *Metodologia della formazione linguistica*, Roma and Bari: Laterza.

——, Calefato, Patrizia and Petrilli, Susan (1994), *Fondamenti di filosofia del linguaggio*, Roma and Bari: Laterza.

Proust, Marcel (1913), *Du côté de chez Swann,* It. tr. by G. Raboni, *Dalla parte di Swann*, vol. 1 of *Alla ricerca del tempo perduto*, ed. L. De Maria, Milano: Mondadori, 1983.

Rabelais, François, *Gargantua e Pantagruele*, Torino: Einaudi, 1973.

Ribeiro, Aileen (1993), 'Utopian Dress', in Ash J. and Wilson E., 1993.

Rich, Adrienne (1985), "Notes towards a politics of location", in Diaz-Diocaretz & Zavala (eds), *Women Feminist Identity and Society in 1980s*, Amsterdam and Philadelphia: John Benjamins.

Rossi-Landi, Ferruccio (1954), "Il concetto di valore", in Bernard et al. 1994.

—— (1985), *Metodica filosofica e scienza dei segni*, Milano: Bompiani.

Sartre, Jean-Paul (1943), *L'essere e il nulla*, Milano: Il Saggiatore, 1968.

Segre, Cesare (1981), voce *Stile*, in *Enciclopedia*, Torino, Einaudi.

Simmel, Georg (1895), *Zur Psychologie der Mode*, It. tr. by D. Formaggio and L. Perucchi, Roma: Editori Riuniti, 1985.

Steele, Valerie (1993), "Chanel in Context", in Ash and Wilson 1993.

—— (1997), *Fetish. Fashion, Sex and Power*, Oxford: Oxford University Press.

Talens, Jenaro (1994), *Escritura contra simulacro*, Documentos de Trabajo, LVI, Valencia: Eutopias.

Tancredi, Paolo (1999), *Sfumature di nero: immagini di decadenza, ironia e desolazione nei video di Madonna*, "Athanor" 1, n.s., Lecce: Manni, 1999.

Tertullian, *De cultu feminarum*, It. tr. by M. Tasinato, *Gli ornamenti delle donne*, Milano: Pratiche, 1987.

Trubeckoj, Nikolaj S (1939), *Fondamenti di fonologia*, Torino: Einaudi, 1971.

Vergani, Guido (1992), *La Sala bianca. Nascita della moda italiana*, ed. G. Malossi, Milano: Electa.

Volli, Ugo (1988), *Contro la moda*, Milano: Feltrinelli.

—— (1992) *Per il politeismo*, Milano: Feltrinelli.

—— (1997), *Fascino*, Milano: Feltrinelli.

—— (1998), *Block-modes*. Milano: Lupetti.

Wark, MacKenzie (1992), "Styling Time", in Calefato 1992.

Wenders, Wim (1998), *The Act of Seeing*, It. tr. *L'atto del vedere*, Milano: Ubulibri.

West, Cornel (1993), *La razza conta*, Milano: Feltrinelli, 1995.

Wittgenstein, Ludwig (1922), *Tractatus logico-philosophicus*, Torino: Einaudi.

Woolf, Virginia (1938), *Le tre ghinee*, Milano: Feltrinelli.

Yourcenar, Marguerite (1951), *Memorie di Adriano*, in Yourcenar, *Opere. Romanzi e racconti*, Milano: Bompiani, 1989.

—— (1983), *Le temps, ce grand sculpteur*, It. tr. by G. Guglielmi, *Il tempo, grande scultore*, Torino: Einaudi, 1985.

Index

(The proper names in the index refer only to the authors cited in the text)